Collected Poems

Collected
Poems

Domenick J. Yezzi, Jr.

ISBN: Softcover   978-1-4363-9691-2

Some poems, in slightly different format appeared in *The Beverwyck*, the literary magazine of Siena College. Other poems were roundly rejected by a number of literary magazines in the 1980s, much to their chagrin today.

A Note on the Typeface: These poems are set in Times New Roman 12, the most commonly used font, which, given the material, seems utterly appropriate.

If you liked this book, you'll probably like the author's CD *The Many Flavors of Dom Yezzi* recorded live at Cove City Sound Studios 8/24/2005; there's no accounting for people's tastes.

This book was printed in the United States of America.

To order additional copies of this book, contact:
Xlibris Corporation
1-888-795-4274
www.Xlibris.com
Orders@Xlibris.com
57419

Contents

Affair with a Stranger 13
Afraid to Move 14
After I've Paused 15
Arena 17
Artist at Work 18
At 70 19
At Mid-winter 20
At the Birth of My Second Daughter 23
At Your Command 24
Ballet School 26
Banking 27
Bassin' 28
Beth 31
Biologically Speaking 32
Bird Hawk 33
The Black Rose 35
Bombarded 37
The Boulder 38
Breaking Free 39
Brook Falls 40
But the Love 43
By Lack of Compass 45
Canoe 46
Carly 47
Carpenter 48
Closed 49
Confessions 50
Consider 51
The Consultation 52
Crows 53
De-planeing 55

Disney 56
Divorced from the Proceedings...................................57
Driving Test..59
The Fog Was Thick...61
For MD..62
For Those Drowning...63
Get the Point?...64
Got a Minute? 65
Here I Go Again 66
Here's How I Want to Hold You 68
Hermit Crab 69
The Highland Diner 70
I am Your Refugee..71
I Don't Doubt...72
I Kiss Your Face..73
I Think I Can Talk 74
If It's Mine to Fill 76
In My Searching...78
I've Spent More 79
Judy Revisited...80
Laundry Day 81
Living in a Flat..83
Lovesick on a Gravel Road 84
The Match..86
Matter of Perception...87
May I? 88
Migration 89
Morning Massacre 90
Much Too Quiet 92
My Catharsis Continues...94
My Heart Here Lies 96
Not to Worry 98
Off-Broadway..99
On a Journey 101
On Page 2 102
One Raging Year...103
Opposites..104
Orbit of My Life..105
Over Hot, Mellow Tea 106

The Pain 108

Plad 109

Plums 110

Poem with Footnotes...112

Portrait...114

Portrait in a Restaurant...115

Potmarked 117

The Propagation of Brooklynites 118

Radical 121

Rainy Day...122

The Reader 123

Religion..126

S. 127

Safety Check 128

The Sea before The Storm 130

The Sea after The Storm 133

Shade Tree..137

Side-tracked 138

Sighing 144

Smiles...145

Sound Bites 146

The Space Between Our Touchings 152

Starting from Scratch..155

Stranger..157

Surgery...159

Thirty-one 160

This Involuntary Twitch 161

This Page..162

Through a Hallway Buzzer 163

Time and Again...165

Time, Gentlemen...166

To: 167

To an Ideal..169

The Trip..170

Two Lives 172

The Two of You...173

U Killed My Cat...174

Upon Building a Dream 177

We Said It Would Be Different 178

We Were Conferring..179
Weekends 180
When I Think of You 181
When Love Shall Rise Up..183
Why the Motorcycle?..184
A Woman Who Can Whistle 185
Wordly Separation..186
Yet Again Today 187
Young, Skinny Kid 188
Your Eyes 190
Your Long Lean Body...191
You're Right 192

**For the women
in my life
who drove me to
poetry and drink**

Author's Note: These poems span over 40 years of my life. When I first decided to compile them, I thought I'd polish and edit them to my current tastes. But as I read them, I realized that each portrays me at a different point in time, and regardless of the quality of the writing, the emotional intensity is evident. So I decided to leave each as I originally wrote it; whether a particular poem is good or bad isn't really relevant to me, but you're free to make your own assessment.

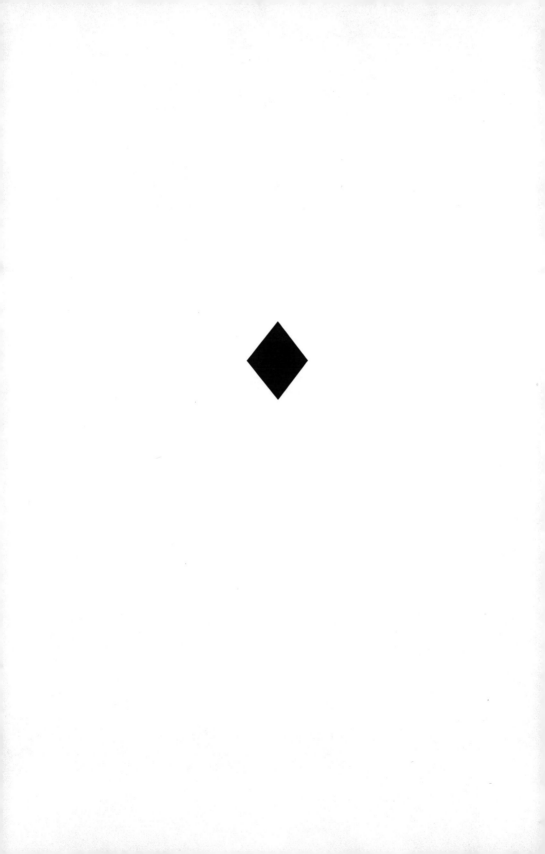

Affair with a Stranger

Crying on the subway? How can that be?
When, at that very selfsame moment, I was loving you . . .
more joyfully than the spring wind dancing down the mountainside
(the leaves applauding as it passes)
and the brightness of my love's joy outshines any gloom!
Dance with my love and cry no more.

You were cold? But this is not possible!
When, at that very selfsame moment, my love was enveloping you . . .
like the warmth from a crackly log-piled fireplace
(tiger-orange—fiercely challenging the cold)
and the intensity of my love's warmth dispels any chill!
Daydream among the coals and be cold no more.

You sideswiped a car? You must be mistaken!
When, at that very selfsame moment, my love was protecting you . . .
more vigilant than a mother guarding her cubs
(with a strength she herself doesn't yet know)
and the keenness of my love's gaze stays all danger!
Cuddle in my lair and fear no more.

When all else fails you
      I'm a crutch,
      I'm the path,
      I'm a new foundation.
You'll find you in me.

Afraid to Move

I'm dreaming
of what it'd be like
to love you; not sex you up,
but good, old-fashioned
attention to detail.

Okay, so the days of me
proved to be as thin
and sheltering as a beggar's coat.

I'm ready now.
Maybe you?
Maybe now?
Until it's time for you to go.

Permit me
to be your release
and thrill.

Help me
to find the key
to free the rush;
let the waterfall roar.

Reduce me
to a slave to your pleasure
(and mine that not taking brings).

Yes, there'll be a time
when I'll need to gently take
my own comfort from you,
but my pendulum can tick for days
before the weight
that pulls at me
needs a lift.

After I've Paused

After I've paused in my rushing
  clankety, clankety, clankety onward
         hell-bound
Hat and face tugged downward,
When I've paused to glance back
  Fugitively   and consider
The words that I've spoken, the poems I've written;
Upon stepping off the deep-rutted road
to consider myself outsiderishly:
I hear a fierce song
  and
     Passion, wanting, longing
  and
    Passion . . .
And I realize it is time for a
     deep-breathed change:

  So let this be light
    and lovely as you;
  leave me, Passion, tonight
    for a joy bursting new.

  I'll bring you another
    nine a.m. present;
  A bright, smiling harbinger
  of you-inspired merriment.

  Love, you fill me
    and warm me inside;
  Your eyes set my mind free—
    only you therein reside.

My lips, with their own will,
      leap, ripe, to a smile;
From the love you instill
        from the thoughts you beguile.

The first one of which
      I'm most keenly aware,
Is how simply I'm enriched,
        by a woman without fanfare.

All good words are yours
      like warm, safe and peace;
Your memory endures
    and this list will increase.

Any maybe someday
      the disjointed praise above,
Will jell and convey
      my deep-dwelling love.

Accept, then, a lover's refrain,
      silly, puppy-dog pants
That try to explain
    a half-way romance
    a love built on chance
    an enchanted circumstance.

Arena

The arena still hasn't surrendered up
　　　all of its old wooden appointments
and the inadequate lighting and dirt floor
　　　make me feel like I've traveled back a half century.

We sit in the very first tier of seats
with only a metal fence tied to the chair railing
between us and the bulls and stallions.

I am surprised at how many people are in the ring:
　　　an announcer, three clowns, two cowboys and two judges.
Two gatekeepers and several riders waiting their turn are watching.
　　　Finally the rider and his bull are released from the holding pen.

The bull kicks and bucks, trying to rid himself
of the strap binding his loins
and the rider who is kicking his shoulders
amid the confusion of yells and the PA system.

The cowboy flops around like a rag toy
and all I can only think of is the back pain
eight seconds of such punishment would inflict on me.

Artist at Work

These marbled eyes were once the color of looking,
Lame as a tree;
Absent were these hands, untried, untouched,
Starved as the dead;
Lips never unfurled, ears never unbridled
Love-proof.

Now they scamper as a crab without its shell,
Or hypnotized by the beam of lit knowledge,
Stand in the field, naked
To the hunter's tired bullet—
A disheveled fox.

So you much come, and finish your love
In the silent day, in the speaking night.
Softly abide with soothing steps
That trample this flesh into your creation.

Then this leisure safety shields you
As the crab its home, as the doe its fawn,
As the fox its coat.
But swear and vow and resolve and die
Into my unborn vision and prayer
And the sun will never crumple your fashions.

At 70

When you set the cruise control at 70
the stripes on the road lengthen
and the gaps
between them
snap at you.

After you've been driving at 70 for a while
you can make out those trees
that are waving in the crowd,
not standing sentinel
along the highway.

When the rhythm of 70 drowns out even the radio
my thoughts slow down
and crystallize on you—
a mantra for the miles yet to come.

At Mid-winter

I touch you much more often
than just the few, infrequent moments
we spend together.
The occasions upon which
the curtain of my subconscious
rises to reveal a spotlit you, glitter-gowned,
are as numerous as notes in a symphony
(but while they're interdependent, you only need you).
If my mind should momentarily
lapse into idleness, it spontaneously (like a spring released)
flies south to you, where it roosts:
needing no trigger, no solenoid
to return once more to the mystical
meaningfulness of you in my life.

So although our togethernesses would seem
too infrequent to maintain
the banks of my love fully flowing,
yet I spend a great deal of my day
holding you, beneath your smile,
and my needing you grows, grows,
grows as steadily as roots
beneath the sidewalk.

It is during these solitudes
that I try to understand your whys,
and oftentimes I understand you
more completely than either of us
cares to acknowledge.

I dissect the anatomy of your casual comments,
because we frequently speak allegorically, in jest, or innuendo,
a tribute to the surface status quo,
but not the most efficient method of
conveying our need
for each other's loving in times of all aloneness.
A few flamboyant words stretch many miles
when the fear of proving
too susceptible a target,
when the fear of being
scorned after stripping
publicly naked,
when the fear of being
only an individual, unesteemed and unaccomplished,
overshadows and distorts our might-have-been communications.

I work hard at maintaining our relationship . . .
harder, perhaps, then even I would ever acknowledge,
and certainly harder than
I would allow you to realize
from a study of my daily activities or soliloquies.
This cold lethargy stems from the
wounds I've had inflected (I must admit:
I raised no hand in self-defense)
although such butcher-shop crudeness
easily becomes assembly-line mundane;
just because they don't bleed readily
doesn't mean these wounds are not deep.

So I shroud my need
for your love to fill these holes in me
with tinkered metal and greasepaint
for fear of invoking your distain
at my flabbiness.

For my wanting you
is a lamprey, who's rasping, rasping teeth
have gouged a raw, deep hole
in my chest, with many jagged, bleeding edges
where the tissue was ripped apart,
to expose the underlying mottled red and white softness.

Sometimes I'm given enough love
to feed both he and I,
but other times, as the thoughts of you
fill my head, my pants,
the pressure mounts dangerously in this vessel,
which already has too many hairline cracks.
(I have my own yellow-tagged relief valves,
and depression is my steam.)

This then, is my poem of love,
down which I've run and rambled
helter-skelter, with a bundle
whose contents are
as confused and illogical as emotion itself,
as waiting and hopeful as the love I nurse.
Though I hide my stoma
and speak as if with authority,
I love you to painfulness.

I often write you verses, but seldom let you read.
My poetry is not perfect, but then neither is my need.

At the Birth of
My Second Daughter

The first time I saw her she was pale blue
as the back of a sun-bleached mussel shell;
Folds of skin on the nape of her head and neck—
Boxer-like,
        soaking wet,
                arm-flinging
                        and beautiful!

She emerged
            without opening speech,
But looked around sightless upside down,
Attended to, all the while, by her court-in-waiting.

Not auspicious:
No multi-colored, feather and polished fanfare
or neon, amplified, spotlit stage.
Just accepting love,
Fresh from the starting block—
                    never questioning—
Warmth radiating from ear to ear.

They bathed her and dressed her
and laid her between us,
Where she began her life-long work
of wondering at all around her,
As she turned more pink   by the moment.
            (the color of questioning)

Not of her own volition this life's begun,
May she never regret or wish the act undone.

At Your Command

At your command:
  "Nothing for you!"
My awareness of my desire doubles,
my need thickens,
and I cannot stop myself
  from stroking this wanting and saying your name.

And you're with me all the more . . .
  as I willingly obey.

But why is this denial so wonderful?
  I am not compelled
  to abide by your commandment;
  you would not catch me
  if I sinned!

Knowing that you own me,
  and can control my only release
with a few words spoken off-handedly on a whim;

Knowing that you can dismiss the pain you're inflicting,
  keeps you constantly on my side,
  fans the dull life within me,
and there is no spark without desire.

And I want more!

Make me climb near the top,
but toss me off,
short of my goal.

Press my body into your service.
         A sacrifice, an offering.
Strip my sanity away
for your amusement.

And when my pant has brought me to my knees,
         a slave at your mercy
Let me realize my desire
         so when we begin again
I can want you all the more.

Ballet School

Performing flock of pigeons
circling above the tenements
and brownstones
in the slightly opaque, ochre Brooklyn air,
where the steady stench of the spewing factories
below the Kosciusko Bridge still permeates, despite the EPA.
A rooftop maestro
conducts this Dance of the Doves:
as they swing into an upward arch
wings beating,
he tosses his arms over his shoulder
and raises to tiptoe as the birds
reach the pinnacle
where he hold his pose,
as they do, then
they, with a unified snap of their wings,
cut left,
to soar downward in this new direction
until once again they plane off,
while the maestro's arms swoop down
to bent knees,
and he pivots to watch their glide
before they all begin their ascent again,
following the path of an imaginary scalloped fringe
that encircles the sky around the rooftop.
And all the while,
they mimic the dancing,
arm-swaying maestro,
who mimics them.

Banking

If a test tube could fix cars and clean,
that's all that would have been required;
it would have been less painful for both of us.

You wanted your babies; you got them.
Everything else was a means to an end.
Having emptied the test tube, you tossed it away;recycling wasn't required!

The anger only erupted after the awakening,
which followed the resignation,
following the pleadings,
after the vows,
built on confidence,
never deserved.

And now the Pavlov-like hate
which can only follow a love
long gone
overpowers even the business of living.

Bassin'

We worked our way
with the breeze and the power of a small electric motor
through a series of small ponds
connected by canals
overhung with branches
drooping Spanish Moss,
where the sun reflected off the ripples we'd made
dancing against the bottom of the canopy of leaves.

The morning was hot and dry,
promising to get worse.

We jigged likely roots and weeds for bass,
picking off one or two from the green water
now and again,
interrupted only by a wisecrack
now and again—
the easy, periodic banter of two who knew enough about
what each was doing
and that each knows what to do,
so as to make talk necessary only for the key issues
of sex and jokes
or for, best of all, jokes about sex.

We passed under a highway
where a guy was casting a bait net in the narrow channel,
mindless of our prop.
We came out into an open lake
where a bevy of fisherman had lined a bank
with bobbers,
the wisdom of the masses
eyeing us quizzically from between their
Marlboro, Mack Trucks and Bass Pro Shop
baseball caps and long necks. We kept going,

heading back into the rushes
where the swallows darted for bugs,
working around us like just so much more
deadwood rising from the swamp.

We'd just settled into a likely drift
when the megaphones from across the lake
crackled to life—
clear as the bright sky in this middle of nowhere—
welcoming the beachgoers to the local talent show,
so important to the parents, so pathetic
to us strangers. Yet one of those kids'll
probably buy me out one day.
But this is no time for being philosophical;
we moved
further away from our invisible irritators
down another canal to other openings in the swamp,
sometimes churning the bottom,
but always finding another opening beyond.

By mid-morning it'd gotten so hot
even the fish couldn't bring themselves to
strike an irksome spinner.
I stripped off my clothes,
told him: "No bassin' here,"
and dove in.

He put his rod butt in a holder,
put his butt down in a seat,
leaned back,
put his feet on the gunwales,
put a long neck in his hand
in his lap, let out a fart,
titled his cap and said "gator"
nodding in the direction behind me.
"Bullshit," I said.
"Your call," he said, and tipped
his bottle back against his lips,
scratching himself with his free hand.

Dammed kid! I took a quick lap
around the boat to prove I wasn't scarred
and got my naked ass out of the opaque soup.

It was pretty much over by then.
We picked up a gar on the way back,
and had to back up to a small bass
who'd wrapped himself around a weed,
but by mid-afternoon we were with the women again,
showered, reserved and chatting incessantly
about nothing I can remember.

Beth

With her tunnel-deep eyes,
with her dark, mother's eyes,
She studies the room as silently
as a Miro staring back
from its museum wall home.

Thumb in mouth,
lips pursed to keep the whole appendage warm,
her eye snaps like a shutter,
focusing as it sweeps the room,
seeing, recording, only half-aware
but never to be forgotten.

I will see this pose
time and again, I know,
at each unfolding of realization.

Soon gum
(worked silently) will replace that thumb . . .
then a nail or two might be decimated from time to time . . .
perhaps, later on, a pinching of the lips
between the teeth
or a scratching of her teeth
across her tongue (or vice versa).

In the end—
a sucking where a tooth once was,
and all the while
still focusing, trying to fathom.

Biologically Speaking

It's easy for a woman to think nothing of being herself.
Her body is no big deal to her
and she doesn't understand the drive inside
me; biologically speaking, the only reason God made me,
and she holds it against me.

God planned many things for her—bringing up kids
and emotions;
for me he planned carrying around the sperm
so there would be change and diversity;
that's it.

Unlike other species, I'm not even the good-looking one.

A woman naked is so hard for a man to accept;
yet so mundane for a woman to be.

No makeup, she figures I'm not even interested;
truth is sexier when not hiding underneath the paint.

Bird Hawk

The broad-tailed hawk,
who rules the sky around here,
has just killed a starling.

Before she came, this snow-covered field
was filled with the chirping of birds.
Now an ear-splitting silence envelopes the air,
like a collapsed tent.

She is magnificent.
Like her sister of the silver dollar
she stands spread-wing,
with her talons
grasping the starling:
no peace branch or arrows-without-bow
for this lady.

Balancing herself on the hard white surface
with her thick wings and tail,
she ignores her thrashing prey
to first survey, challengingly,
the surrounding sky and tree line.

Her eyes are pure gold,
fixed in their sockets
by the master jeweler.
They have their own brown-sparkled life.

She turns her attention to the captured bird
stretched beneath her
with one leg flaying wildly in the air.
A few quick jabs to the chest, and the starling—
who never was a match—is silent.

With an audible pounding of air and wings
the hawk is gone,
but the silence of her worship
remains.

The Black Rose

By a late-afternoon, sun-descending lake,
two to-be lovers
envelope each other on a too-old park bench
probing with words, arms and lips
the unfocused boundaries of this shiny-new universe.

They've come each from their own darkness,
packing the dreams they believed they'd need
not realizing what they'd require for this journey
they'd already given each other,
wrapped, ready to open.

She lays her head back,
lips parted,
seemingly ready to bite in.
Her hair falls aside,
revealing a fresh oval beauty
that radiates as a warm flush rushes in
to replace the numbing coolness
which had been her deft defense.

For them, the years have dropped away,
shattering; a no-longer-needed casing.
When he looks at her, she looks straight back—
there's no reason to pretend—
but she isn't prepared for his smile,
and at first she wonders;
until she recognizes it as genuine;
no puppies here, just a knowing adoration.

The infrequent, intruding tourists—
chatting too loud, tossing their trash—
don't feel the tremor of the moment's movement,
as the past rumbles down into the chasm,
leaving the linked lovers
standing on the future rim.

And she is the defining one;
she asks: "Will you make love to me?"
And he feels he is a black rose
finally unfolding, shimmering
in a warmth
that has been too long in coming.

Bombarded

Bombarded by the surreal sounds and sights of the subway
people escape into their iPods and newspapers:
Roaring, clanking, preaching about the lord,
dancing or singing for a buck,
water-dripping
mouse and rat scurrying.

You drop in (to my mind) unexpectedly.
How do you do that?
The other faces disappear.

The Boulder

Your life's task has been chosen for you.
We are giving you this crystal wine glass.
With it,
remove this boulder
that is blocking the mouth of the cave,
and you will be free.

This boulder is as large
as a nursemaid on a shopping spree
in the middle of winter.

I stand behind this impediment
unable to circumambulate it
not knowing if it is only the tip of an iceberg.

I fill my glass
and, summing all my strength,
dash the water mightily against the
smooth surface of the stone.

The water rolls off the stone
and seeps into the places I've never been.

Each day my mentors come back to inspect my progress.

Breaking Free

It's her eyes that keep me coming home.

I join four friends for drinks after working all week.
We huddle around a too-small table
and begin by trading intentionally amazing, exaggerated stories.
But soon we are telling the truths
you can only tell infrequent friends.
They touch me to impart emphasis,
but they are all beautiful women,
and I'm much too weak for their touches.

It's been almost a year since I've been intimate with a woman.
So I ache at the charge in each touch,
all too aware of my hard reaction.
But nothing comes of our tete-a-tete, each wondering why.
Again.

Going home I vow not to.
I know I must start a new life-climb one more time.
And yet I pull into the driveway.

It's my daughter's eyes looking into me,
waiting for my rejection to break the calm
that keeps me under the surface.

Her bravado can't mask how vulnerable she is.
Her eyes search mine,
asking questions.
I'm not stronger than her weakness.

It's the returning home that so unforgiving.

Brook Falls

At the crest,
the brook is pushed
through a narrow slit
between two
guardian boulders.
Like ice water
from a waiter's pitcher
it arcs through the air,
leaping free
of the mountain,
in a solid, curling,
believe-you-can-see-through-it
braided rope,
and plunges deeply
into a pool
where it rises again smoothly
to the edge
and is split by a prow-rock
into a right and left falls
that bounce
in white excitement
(after so many miles
          of just weaving around
                  on a bed of rocks),

off the ridges
it hasn't yet worn away,
but will,
like a woman
civilizing her husband.

Lazily then, it broadens out to smoothly and evenly cover
the more irregular surface of a flat, worn limestone shelf,
seeking an easy passage, so you barely know it's there,
except for an inch or two of flickeringness
you can't quite focus through.

Nonstop,
      the once-Brook,
            now Falls,
plunges,
        meanders, bubbles, flows
and cascades
      down 250 feet
of ridges,
      pools,
         and just plain cliff
              -face.

On some shelves you can work your way across
by carefully   selecting
     the high points   where the   harder rock
has   not yet   succumbed   to the brook's
incessant   efforts.

Looking
down from
some ridges
you believe you could leap
               to the other side,
if you were only a few years younger,
had a woman worthy of the display,
or were, like Pan, half-goat, or half-cocked.

Sometimes the flow is smooth
like an O in your mouth,
the water clear and thin.
In other places it forms pools
where small, polished stones have
collected—the stream's valuables—
fresh from the jeweler's tumbler.

Under the overhangs by the banks
mud swirls
           in an endless
                  eddy,
          now tan,
      now brown,
now twist,
a puddle in which the child in the brook may play.

The rock face is mostly clean,
and speckled tan,
except where the Spring melt and Autumn rains,
or the splashes   the   —sided
           from   one   onslaught
of the stubborn, but submissive, limestone below,
have allowed moss to gain a foothold.

No fish or plant grows here,
the water and rock being sufficient unto themselves.

At the base, in the meadow,
where the falls has concluded its rush for attention,
people lounge in the state park,
having paid their money to park
(their cars, and by extrapolating
the interior of their cars, themselves)
throwing Frisbees, listening to radios,
eating, reading, drinking and talking,
while the sensible brook reemerges,
and finds its way to the stoic river
where it loses its identity
amid the relations of other brooks.

But the Love

But the love,
        now Our Love,
                was not satisfied
To be a little Suzy Blackeye, but wanted to be
        A full-grown Sunflower.
And the pain of growing was in my face:
And the pain of growing was in Her face.

Please god, no more pain for Her:
        Don't make me the cause of Her misery,
        who wants to be the presence of joy!

But—instead:
        Longings unfulfilled, beyond the limits of reason.
        Confusion, where wisdom should prevail.

The time we shared together,
        That brief stopping of the clock—
Was more beautiful than the dawn after the rain.
        But a full night's sleep is needed
To appreciate the meaning of the sun rising;
        Let my smile guide you to a restful sleep!

Certainly I want all of you!
        Wanted it a continent ago,
                when I refused you,
Just as you wanted all of me
        In that enduring absence of time,
                when you refused me.

Please:
      Let these longings and refusals
                    be our Bond.
Which we satisfy by giving all we can
                    of what we are allowed to give!
The world is only physical—
              it cannot stand between thoughts
      exchanged honestly.

Let me be what you need me to be
      When you want me to be it:
         Your Joy,
            Your Strength,
                  Your Confidant,
I stand ready and willing . . . At Your Call.

If I can be no more than your sedative,
      Then let me be that . . . and be troubled in your mind no longer.

Let me be everything you need for peace . . . Always!

By Lack of Compass

My north star drifts across the night.
Either I must choose a new star
or go in a direction not of my own choosing.
Neither alternative appeals;
Perhaps I'll split the difference
and cross a field between.

This star was axiomatic
yet it's changed.
If this rule then is for breaking,
are the fences bordering this field for scaling?
And how many slats must be removed
from a mile-long fence,
to enable me to slip through?
How many out of the fence
built by you?

I will take my hammer to them . . .

Canoe

I took the canoe today
to Hidden Lakes,
          so full of lily pads
No boats can go there
            save canoes.
The entrance is a narrow channel between two willows.
And there,
      as I quietly slid among
Yellow and white flowers,
            bees and frogs,
The bottom of the canoe
rasped by the leaves of the plants,

I stopped and thought
and the usual conflicts assaulted me.

I watched, and when the battle was over,
life was given to two halves of my mind
where only one had existed before.

Carly

I admit it's been a while
Since I've felt the need to write,
But then again, I haven't been this troubled in a while.

I've been busy trying to be me,
Someone I haven't known for too many years,
Or at least I think it's me I'm being.

At first I tried a companion,
Thinking other women might not be as choking,
But they are.
Must come with the breed.
And now I know what I cherish most
Is my solitude at night.

But now you want to make plans,
And you've hurt me,
Because I'm no longer at your beck and call.
It's not your fault,
You haven't asked it of me.

So you've got your project
And you want me to set it up for you.
I can do that.
But I want to be more than your emissary.
I need to be in the trenches with you.

But this, too, is my fault.
I've made commitments I'm compelled to keep,
A nasty habit I'm not able to break.

And you never asked for the help anyway.

Carpenter

Half-breath from metal tanks is fed me
all but one seated knowledge. Silver around
my neck may hand, but solid gold upon my
finger sparkles.
For who would tell me wicker baskets
could not hold leaves of unbleached knowledge,
nor cigarettes hold thoughts and words, until my polished shadow
be cut by sun?
For who could tell me she would be there,
to smash my tortured hand before its fruitless climax,
to take an axe upon my polished shadow—in need of hand
and saw and plane?

Closed

They lock the beaches in my town at night.
That just doesn't seem right somehow;
how can lovers sit on the sand and watch the sun rise?
But the signs say "No Loitering".

They've blocked the sky at night in my town.
That just doesn't seem right somehow;
how can lovers moon at the moon in October?
But the lights block the stars so they can't be seen.

They've closed the parks in my town.
That just doesn't seem right somehow;
how do the raccoons, deer and their lovers know to say out?
But the signs say "Closed at Dusk".

Confessions

The confessions I disguise as poems!
They're little more than plain talk
Separated, hyphenated, interjected,
Love hidden among the free flowing stanzas.
A literature born of desire!

My first day away was as painful
As any day I choose to remember.
The longings I have now for you
Are sometimes too strong to quench.
They suck my strength,
And leave my body shaking, sighing.

My first night of dreams . . .
                     What marvelous dreams.
There in a room I've yet to see;
There, where only the bed matters;
I stand before you—
                 Cleopatra on her chaise,
And deliberately remove my clothing
Baring myself for you to view
(a little more than self-consciously).

At your command I turn
Like a pedestalled automobile at the World's Fair
The flaccidness leaving me
As each new degree of the compass is completed,
Till, full circle,
I'm pointed in the right direction.

You lay back languishing,
As I methodically unbutton and kiss,
Letting my lips and tongue
Do the additional work
my hands are too occupied to pursue.

Consider

I can think of no romantic or poetical
way of saying I love you.
Consider:

Your voice on the telephone is enough
to make me put my feet up on the desk
and forget my work.
I become a boy again,
laughing and joking.

I think I could talk to you
for hours and never get bored.

Seeking you takes all the pain away.

The Consultation

Eye-to-eye, in a consultation
on the difficulties of associating
the correct databases and disk space
I suddenly smile.
I see the question in your eyes:
Did I say something inane?
Do you see an obvious solution I've missed?

But rather than raise the question
you continue outlining the situation,
which is just as well.
Because how could I explain
without repercussion?
The reason I'm smiling is:
You're beautiful.

Crows

I used to think crows are smart.
I never saw an animal
that had figured out all about cars
except for crows.
Probably got that smart
watching and waiting for
animals too stupid to not get hit.

I can't tell you the number of times
I've come bearing down on a crow
picking over some delicacy in the middle of the road
only to watch him calmly
—at the last minute—
cross over to the other side of the
yellow line and politely wait while I drove by.

Why, they're even smart enough to use the
X'ed out triangles in the Y's in the road.

But I guess they're not smarter
than gulls.

Saw a crow today
trying to make a meal
out of a mussel, a-la-gull.

I guess while he was waiting for
a squirrel or possum or raccoon
not to make it across the road
he must have been watching a gull
drop a mussel or two to eat.

Guess he never figured out how to
hover, however,
because he found himself a mussel
in the reeds
and then stood
on the dock
and dropped it from knee-high again and again.
The mussel didn't much care.
Probably had a bad headache, though.

Didn't think crows got mad,
but I swear this one did,
slamming the mussel down by the beard
with a flick of his head.
Probably got his own headache.

He's gonna have to hang
around the beach a while longer
before he gets this one right.

De-planeing

The endless stream of de-planeing passengers
(a procession of Volkswagen-exiting, makeup-less clowns)
parts
and suddenly you are there
standing apart from the grey mob
fresh and glowing
and my doubts are cast away.

Our coming and going
has brought us closer together.

Disney

This forced idleness

This obligatory teaching of the children
about cartoon characters no longer
relevant to their generation

This scheduling of events and rushing
to see things

This?

Divorced from the Proceedings

Eerie transition between conclusion
of day and commencement of night
(Neither sun nor moon is visible overhead,
and the pane's grey lights on either hand
don't meet in the middle of the sky)
Made more strange
by the bones of winter supporting the horizon—
the supplanting skeletons of trees
hung by their thumbs.

Melancholy clings to me like shrinkwrap
as if I were laid to rest
in a green Styrofoam tray—
a bond I am helpless to break,
as impenetrable as
Christmas wrapping paper.

Caught in the tube of a funhouse tumbler
revolving:
Never mind comparing me to the world around—
I'm insignificant enough just being compared
to my own kind.

Woman dressed as precisely
as a full page, color, glossy advertisement
walks though unabashed
by the floor revolving.
Her face is covered with the wrinkles of
bitching,
pulling, pulling the skin into the
mouth and down the throat.

Am I the only human estranged
by my own lack of self-actualization

in this ear-humming world?
The wide-awake green road signs
measure the distance
to the end of the silly half-sideways dance
in rods and furlongs.

A thoroughbred whispers from
where I cannot see him, that
40 rods = I furlong.
I still do not know how far
I must travel back to reality.

The strangeness bursts buzzing
into full purple.

Driving Test

On the eve of my sister's driving test
She felt she needed a little more practice,
Because she wanted to look her best
But wasn't yet confident in our parent's new car.

So I offered to take her for a ride,
And we left in the little green Nash Rambler.
If I'd said it was old I would have lied:
It was extremely old and not too solid.

My sister was fine, until, at one point,
She signaled for a left and proceeded to turn right.
Well, the guy behind got his nose out of joint,
Because he'd started to accelerate to pass on that side.

He laid on the horn and sis froze at the wheel,
She stepped on the gas and kept turning, turning,
I'm not sure how, but that automobile
Managed not to flip, though it had the right to.

What stopped us was the rear of a van
Parked at the curb without its brake on,
And it popped out of gear when it met our sedan
And rolled up the lawn of a house right there.

It tapped the house gently and started back down.
When it hit the Rambler it only bounced once,
Causing a liquid to drip out that looked kind of brown,
And steam to pour out where the radiator had been.

After it was all over;
After my sister stopped crying
        and remembered to shut off the engine;
After the steam had cleared;
After the homeowner had stopped lamenting his lawn;
After the three police cars had all left;
After the van driver had finished reporting to his boss,
        and taken the rest of the day off;
After my father had stopped shaking his head
        and finished selling the car to a junk dealer;
After the insurance company had decided
        how much to raise our premium;
After all this:
        it was three years before my sister got her license.

So on the eve of your driving test
I'll not be offering you any sage advice,
But wish you "Good Luck" (this part's not in jest)
And hope you don't ever need to use the luck.

The Fog Was Thick

The fog was thick:
shopping mall

We can make it (4 tracks)
Come on, hesitate and go

Shopping cart
Years of commuting
Not the right sound
thumping

body rolls down 12 cars
What can you expect to find?
What goes through his mind as he walks down the train
thinking what will it be, Kid, Deer?
Dark as is.
Did they stop trains on Track 3 okay?

Engineer waits with the vision of the figure and his heart

The reaction of Passengers:
silly grinning
signing
confused and concerned
Did they have any packages?

One engineer to the other: "Billy, you okay?"
several times
Thinking: glad it's not me.
How do you handle?
"Got it, Billy. He's under the last car."

Nothing in the papers
Rumors

Next night different train, different crew

For MD

She matter-of-factly recites her poems.
She speaks of changes and hardships,
of decisions and turning-aways,
of start-overs and never-have-beens,
as if we've all had the guts to do the same
and so would understand what she has to say.

This slim, smiling, full
person
is more determined,
has fewer trepidations,
than I
of my size and sway.

Fulfillment has its own way of finding you.

For Those Drowning

You fool, little Sister, you've wasted your life away!
Sitting on your behind, crouched in the corner,
Trying to look as small as a mouse in a room full of cats.
Do you think your kind can survive, and if so, how much longer?

What a waste of your mind—all you do is repeat
Your mystical, magical, mythical chants
In traditional, time-honored sequence and cadence,
While most passers-by give you barely a glance.

How can that little brown bowl ever repay you
For the time that you gave up, hiding away
Behind rosary beads, crosses and shapeless brown clothes—
Never giving, never thinking, never working, one day.

I know you'll tell me of love and humility,
But love of god is love of nothing,
And humility is only learned by having tried and failed
Such bullshit only leaves me cursing.

I see you take, but what do you have to give?
You prey on other people's guilts and fears,
And the money you've begged is soiled and tainted
By blood, by loathing, by cheating, by tears.

And you and all those like you who need to survive
By hiding and hoping for some future relief
Would be sorely disappointed if it were possible to know
After you're dead there'll be nothing left of your belief.

Get the Point?

EVERYTHING:
>How you clip your toenails . . .
>The flavor jelly you prefer . . .
>If your slip has a hole in it . . .

NOT JUST:
>The times you tripped and fell . . .
>The name of every friend you lost . . .
>Who you love and don't love . . .

OR IF:
>Those you love love you . . .
>Your dreams are good or bad . . .
>You've filled any of the emptiness inside you . . .

BUT ALSO:
>The titles of every book you've read . . .
>Every bedroom you've ever slept in . . .
>Every man you've ever known . . .

AND THEN:
>That wouldn't be enough . . .
>It would only be too little . . .
>This would just be a beginning . . .

FOR THERE'S STILL:
>The pictures you remember . . .
>The dolls you hugged . . .
>The days you wandered the garden picking flowers . . .

Every forest on earth
would have to be converted
>>to paper
before I'd finish
listing all the facts
>of you
I wish to know.

Got a Minute?

It started as a game . . . our secret
     small exploratory excursions into regions we dared to reveal.
It grew into the realization
     of how unique a woman you are:
                 light touches,
                    teasing glimpses,

Shared thoughts,
       and
        too-easy revelations.

Coming face-to-face with yearnings held inside before
     saying the things I've never told anyone.

And what do I want to say to you?
     It will be long, there's so much.

Got a minute?

Here I Go Again

I

And here I go again—Will you look at me, please!
Like a time-tired trawler struggling against seething seas—
With the waves first washing over my sun-blistered bow
And then turning to thrash in my wake; and now
Jumping in a froth, in angry fist-shaking peaks,
Spitting foam. As doubting and dreading the cabin creaks,
The floorboards feel still softer beneath my boat shoes.
The radio beckons: "Broadcast—Tell them: 'Save Our Souls',"
But compulsive as my compass I steer nearly into the storm,
Working my hands on the wheel in an effort to keep them warm.
Starboard a bright blazing light tempts me to change course
But my hull cannot stand side-smashing shots of such force.

II

And I wonder how I ever got so lost, after all these years.
I was to have sought and found, to have accomplished, and to have
drowned
My doubts by how. Instead I still fight my freely following tears
Who, like jello in a mold, fill the cracks in all my moods
And have just as much backbone.
And if I, every now and then, like a comic book hero,
Topple them and force them to hide, stand over them with legs planted
wide,
My yearnings laugh and yowl. With my confidence approaching zero
I'm forced to scratch and claw and patch and brace—and build
A small mud house for myself.
Will this be all—to fear and want: be never satisfied or unafraid?
To be dreadfully driven, to endlessly work, with no time given
Over to rest? Must these everlasting longings be always obeyed
Who boil in my brain, spit on my fire, at the time when only a
Simmer should remain?

III

Even now, at the end of this storm, the water is in motion:
The surface is alive with the swirls of deep traveling animals,
The peaks and valleys are aglow in the albedo of the sun.
Rocking in the waves and resting are a ship's worth of gulls—
They'd followed this far before the cook ran out of scraps for them.
And here and there whitecaps of foam jump skyward,
Like the snow from the peaks reaching down to kiss the hem
Of the skirts of blue grass with which the mountains are gird.
And the orange-haired head of the freckled imp of a sun
Peaks over the horizon mischievously to see what I'm doing;
He watches me writing of love and the rare phenomenon
That is you, and he tires but cannot understand my ruing
Your absence, for he sees you each day. All around me is action,
And if you were but here this liveliness would not have me so undone.

IV

The storm on the sea and the storm in my mind
Have played themselves out now; laid down to rest
And the world all around has burst forth like crocuses in spring.
Within minutes you'd never have known a
Storm was here—all is back to normal.
Now my doubts turn to needs as I
Long for my own beauty, and I
Take up my clipboard, a chart pencil, and begin to write anew.

Here's How I Want to Hold You

Here's how I want to hold you:
        all skin, curled,
slightly damp against me, with your hand resting
        where you last touched me,
feeling free to rub the hair on my chest.

Here's how I want you to hold me:
        with your fingers wrapped in my hair,
pulling my face deeper into you.

Hermit Crab

Like a hermit crab, ashamed
—scurrying among the weeds—
I move from shell to shell,
picking each clean,
trying to find a home.

And having tired of this one
—though it looked good when I picked it up—
and finding I'm no more comfortable with my newest,
I move on to pick over another,
not having learned
you can never fully clean up behind someone else.

The Highland Diner

She looked directly at me and I looked directly at her
and the look passed between us.

We kept glancing at each other openly
each time she passed through the swinging kitchen
door, yelling an order or picking one up:
her blond, pulled-back-in-disarray hair,
her dark, full eyebrows framing the question;
her beauty unquestionable.

I take an unneeded trip to the men's room to walk past her
as she counts her tips at the counter.
We look at each other one more time,
knowing the time.

I get back on my motorcycle and ride.

I am Your Refugee

I am your refugee,
      vulnerable from neglect,
            seeking a shelter of love.

I am your brothel,
      explore my rooms,
            they have many different pleasures and faces.

Rub me up and down,
      find my positive charge:
            the arc will light the years of darkness.

I Don't Doubt

I don't doubt your mother was right:
  I'm sure you must have been
    The most beautiful baby ever born to woman
You're the most beautiful woman ever born to baby
   And although the joke might be a poor one
    I'd like to try the babying, nevertheless.
This is not to say I think you're a baby
   You're a strong, resilient woman
    Which is the only way I could love you.
For beauty is enhanced when it is strong
   And independence breeds a loveliness all its own,
    And being tough doesn't mean the fabric can't be elegant
And tomboys grow the firmest legs!

I Kiss Your Face

I kiss your face,
             your neck,
                    your breasts.

I remove your pants,
My hands sliding down your legs.
And starting at your feet,
I nibble my way up the
Insides of your smooth-skinned legs,
Until I bury my face
Between your legs,
Your soft, tender thighs around my head,
And my arms around them,
With my hands struggling to reach your breasts.

I imagine you taste salty,
And as bitter-sweet as this dream/poem.

I stay in this position
For the balance of my dream.
Tasting you, and smelling you,
And never going any further.
Oh, sometimes I turn you over,
And pursue the same tactics from behind,
But in all my feeling,
             kissing,
                    touching,
                           biting,
I never try to consummate
             my dream.

What do you think, doctor?

I Think I Can Talk

I think I can talk
about my loss of control now,
although I fear my explanation
will sound trite and contrived.

I felt light-headed
as if I were hyperventilating (on loving you)
weak, exhausted—
I could not control
my heart, my lungs
even my eyes blurred:
a total emotional collapse,
but no frustration.

"Freaked out"
        the kids might say
"Strung out"
        the street-wise might correct them
"Mild heart attack"
        the doctor would diagnose
"Lost his sense of equilibrium"
        the lawyers would declare
"Need heap strong medicine"
        the Indian Chief would command
"Hung-up"
        the butcher might have confided
"Over-cooked"
        the baker would have sobbed
"Burnt at both ends"
        the candlestick maker might have lamented

"Tell me"
the psychiatrist asks
"Have you ever OD'ed
because of a woman
before?

"I guess I had a few too many
kisses"
I confess,
and to myself I answer
No, never!
Was I wrong?
I guess I shouldn't have
gotten so involved
knowing
even as I might just be attaining top speed
that I'd have to reverse my engines
full speed astern.

But I'd run the risk
again
and again
and only just now
am I beginning to realize
I am your addict.

If It's Mine to Fill

If it's mine to fill—
    Let me fill it with the joy of our miracle:
The spontaneity of my smile at your sight is my witness!

Between the void I came from, happily,
And the nothingness I'm racing towards, recklessly,
I've been given a chance (while we're together) to
    Cast off my clothing, and
    Revel in the freedom of the honesty I've found within me:
I have never before been truthful (even to myself),
And now that I have—
    Happiness has been my reward.

By why must you ask: Why?
Do you doubt yourself still?
Do you think that when I tell you about
    your beauty, about
        the pleasures of conversing and laughing with you, about
            the mournful gazes of so many others like me,
That I am only romanticizing as a lover would?
    Please,
I'm much too practical to waste time daydreaming!

Lecture: We all fall into the syndrome
    of viewing ourselves through our pasts:
    of tainting what we are with the knowledge
    of what we have been—
And all the while, being overcritical!

I care not to know what you were . . .
This moment is my starting point . . .
I proceed from here—
    forward,
        not backward.

Look at what you have become:
      This is the you I know!
      This is the you I've come to love!
      This is the Why:
            In you is strength I admire!
            About you is beauty I covet!
            Over you is gaiety I cherish!
            Within you is passion I desire!
Look me in the eyes and I am filled with the realization of
      All the worldliness you represent.

You deserve to be loved
      like any hand-crafted work of art:
and how often is the artist and his art
      one and the same?

This love of mine is just beginning . . .

In My Searching

In my searching I've raced to showcase beauties
but I've learned they need to keep their distance;
I don't want to see the fuzz on their stockings.

But yours is effortless beauty
framed by the color of passion.

Before I go up in flames

                             over you

I'm ready to go down in flames

                             with you.

I've Spent More . . .

I've spent more than I should have
on wistful, mellowing paintings,
soaring bronze sculptures,
potentially vestal vases,
museum tickets

seeking beauty.
Yet what these artists
paint, splash, sculpt, shape, grotesque, love
is you, woman,
and I, like them, never tire

seeing you naked.
Pretty equals checking off the attributes,
breast roundness, nipple geometry,
lean legs rising to a mount of soft hair;
fit the pieces together for your

work of art.
Beauty is
the imperfections that create fascination.

Judy Revisited

Age has settled so softly and lovely on you
like petals opening on a rose
revealing a softer, less startling red.

I tossed and turned and walked the house.
Through shear curtains billowing in the breeze
I keep seeing your face across the table.

Laundry Day

This bum
with his moist, moldy, mottled bundle
          clasped between his arms
(locked dirty hands   to dirty wrists),
strays down the street,
not gazing at even the things his eyes see.

His outfit is uniform in color,
somewhere between olive drab and brown
—the natural colors of this city's camouflage.
He wears a jacket which reaches only to his waist
(yet I am more bothered by the cold of the evening
in my long-lined coat that he).
His distinguishing feature—
the bright, startlingly blue eyes
beneath the security guard's cap he sports.

Somehow, his hair halos around his head
and face in fine strands
hanging in a fetching,
curving inward sweep at his collar to form a bowl.
The beard is only a few week's
growth. It is constantly this length.

He stops were he always does,
where the sidewalk curb is worn away to street level
and two side-by-side manhole covers
billow steam freely.

On one he begins to lay out his laundry neatly.
He appears to have equal amounts of
male and female clothing.

He performs this housekeeping leisurely
as if he holds a union card,
turning a piece sideways sometimes
to get it just right, or turning it inside out.

At last he unpacks a folded cardboard box
which he sets up over the other manhole cover
and crawls under and goes to sleep.

Living in a Flat

To this handled paper cup
(with the gap-tooth blue trim
that does not quite meet itself)
holding instant coffee
powdered milk
and artificial sweetener
in proportions of my own choosing,
I add hot water
directly from the tap
and stir it with a
thin, gay plastic straw.

A tan frothy foam
covers the difference
between the thick liquid and the rolled brim.

I drink the viscous result:
It tastes like my life.

In the end:
I will piss away the coffee;
I will fold and throw away the cup;
I will chew and separate and bend
        and discard the striped straw.

Perhaps next time
I'll get a B, SC, C, S cover
and take it with me.

Lovesick on a Gravel Road

Lovesick on a gravel road:
I remember being
Wrapped in the heavy blue charisma
Of our night,
In the shelter of a melancholy mountain,
Beneath a sky so full of stars
The moon's absence was unnoticed,
For the sky was as an endless dawn.

I'll never be sure, my love,
Whether the forest respected my desire for silence,
Or if my numb mind shut out all sounds of living,
But I heard only the sound of a young bond,
Root-like, growing,
Encircling us,
Drawing us together.

And I remember, too,
Holding fiercely onto the moment, onto you:
With passion as red
As the immense white heat burning behind my closed eyelids,
With a white-knuckled grasp,
With a wide-opened body, an eager receptacle
Soaking up your essence
Pressing you, unprotected—
Probing you like space-radar—
Searching for the slightest vibration
To add to the store of marvels
I've named You.

But I remember best
This portrait of you:
      The thin, wide smile,
           Your most beautiful asset;
      The sad, tired eyes,
           Changing colors to suit your moods;
      Your constant fragrance,
           Distinct, memory-jogging.

In a neither world
So very soft, round and silent.

The Match

Two pawns stand supporting each other
not quite daring to face the quiet queen
who wields a terrible scepter
hand-crafted of white dollies and pink crepe.

This one moves up,
stands beside the oblivious other.
"For me to make progress you must
take this chance"
he says to her who stands closer to the monarch.

The other does not complain
but forces a serious smile.

The queen grins broadly within her mask.
No need to smite this pawn!
As for the brief be-knighted bold one . . .
his rapid-beating time will come!

Matter of Perception

It's a matter of perception: You think my smiling
Means I am not serious—Does that one preclude the other?
If I am to truly mean what I say, must I frown?

I cannot contain my happiness when given the opportunity
To be in your presence—Not every man is so lucky!
I can tolerate no problems when I am with you.

I must smile when you compliment me,
Because I strive so hard for your approval
I do not care to seek the approval of others.

If you were to peel this onion layer by layer
Each skin would be transparent and identical—
Each would be smiling for you, hoping for a smile in return.

May I?

Here I am
betwixt and between
waiting for the culmination
of something I'd started 25 years ago,
but not quite ready to start over again.

There you are
committed,
with a longer row to hoe than mine.
I have time, can I spell you?

May I offer you the alternative
you want but didn't know then?
Tell me,
it'll be ours to keep.

Use me,
teach me what you want.
I promise to deliver.

Migration

The calling cries echo across the sky
as this endless column of birds
passes across the gap
the path has made in the trees above me.

As wide as a French boulevard,
the members of this flight
to their wintering grounds
are the mottled black of starlings in the fall.

Screeching, looking only at the
tail feathers of the bird in front
they continue across the sky
heading north by west.

Somewhere up ahead the procession
is turning more westward
and the column starts shifting sideways
in that direction,
but never does the column stop.

Morning Massacre

                                        In the bight
Formed by this beach and the spit that runs nearly parallel to it
(Thinking itself a long shore bar and the water between a lagoon)
                                        A massacre has occurred.

                                        The bend is choked
With Ulva that the cold and old age has loosened from the bottom.
It has rolled itself into large balls, long ropes and cables
                                        That stretch up onto the
                                        beach

                                        Like the mooring lines of
                                        the sea.
There the sun (once life, now death) has bleached it into dirty toilet paper
And there a host of brand-new flies buzz in figure eights and circles,
                                        Heard more than seen.

                                        Death stalks behind
This entanglement of green, on the leeward shore of the bar—
Snappers sparkle in and out of a school of young mummichugs
                                        Who leap skyward, praying.

                                        Floating tail down in the
                                        mass
Of shinning, dark green, pulsating lettuce (the sea's motion giving them life)
Are fifty or more brittle, light ban, no-bigger-than-your-fist,
                                        Young-of-the-year
                                        horseshoe crabs.

                                        Has disease killed them?
Were they caught by the seaweed rolling snowball-like to the beach?
Did the competition for food become too severe, or has the cold
                                        Caught them too close to
                                        shore?

It must have been the cold.
The shore is littered with the discarded feathers of molted birds,
And close by a small group of terns huddles in the midst of
A large gathering of herring
gulls.

Among them some young
gulls
Have already changed to their brown, sun-warming winter armament.
These youngsters are the first to fly off at the sight of me.
Some others have seen me
before—

These stay where they are.
As I pass by the flock, two mute swans come about in the shallows silently
And begin to follow me, paddling through the seaweed, nonchalantly
Selecting the choicest Ulva

For their breakfast.
They are oblivious to the dead horseshoe crabs, and the dying
Mummichugs in the shallows behind them in their hunger to sustain
Their own living.

The female comes ashore,
stands by me—
Stretching, preening, eyeing me in hopes of a change of diet.
I have nothing but a lukewarm cup of coffee, so we both turn away.
Neither of us can live on
death.

Much Too Quiet

The words I write are Johnny-pump mute!
Sterile as the longing within—
A bag lady poet am I, am I,
Wandering waspishly down ragtag streets,
Mumbling my shabby poems aloud—
A column of manhole-cover steam
Emanating from my mouth, expansive but
Dissipating unnoticed!

Gaze
into my brown-walled bag,
Where my rubble of prisoners,
this menagerie,
Has lined up and claimed to be a unity!
Damn it—they don't fit—god damn it! god damn it!
See—I string them along:
I connive, I cajole, I contort;
And when they're all arranged in stanzas . . .
When they're size-placed and uniform . . .
Then they're still only an unquarried pile
Of bangs, buzzes and beeps.

Nouns to the left of me!
Verbs to the right of me!
Adjectives and adverbs,
Hither and yonder:
A field full of scampering goats
They refuse to be herded
by the black-robed nuns,
Who hold on high
New Year's Eve dime-store metal clickers
each in the shape of a croaking frog.

Come together! Form a poem! Fill this
abyss

deep	
deep	into
	which
e	my
m	breath
p	is
t	being
y	sucked

By the icy vacuum in the pit of my chest.
The pain is a bittersweet,
lingering violin after a crescendo,
whose music hums on long after
the strings have
stopped
quivering—
leaving only my mind quivering.

And so each poem leaves a silence behind
as loud as the words on this page.

My Catharsis Continues

As I come to grips
and wrestle with the realization
my life will not follow the path to the sunset
I'd planned,
I purge it of the trappings
I'd collected
to anchor and hold me steady
(now just so much baggage)
and prepare myself for change.

Today I filled my truck twice
with the now-junk I'd stored in anticipation of helping
my children build separate lives as I did
(Who would want to?)
by scrapping together what's needed
from the spare parts of other's lives.

They knew I no longer needed to make-do
long before I did,
buying new while I was still patching
and bastard-rigging.

Now I've thrown away twenty years
of collected lobster pot buoys of all colors and designs,
parts for cars I no longer own,
the legs of a ping-pong table,
and hair dryers, phones and radios
I was going to combine the working parts
of some day and resurrect.

The first load goes into the waste pit,
and it's a waste I no longer feel,
as I free myself of my responsibility
to not waste what I have the power to save.

I no longer wish to save anything but myself.

On my second trip to the dump, I bring a full
load of metal to the metals-only bin.
A bent old man backs his matching pickup
next to mine. Out of habit
he's wearing his blue work clothes and boots.
He eyes the three single-piston engines
lying in the bed of my truck
and asks me if he can have them.
I understand. I say yes.

But he's worried they'll kick us out
if we make the switch now;
you're not allowed to take things away,
only leave them. Even a dump
takes comfort in its possessions.

So we meet outside the gates
and I hoist the engines
on top of the framing he didn't unload
he was so anxious I might change my mind
if he took the time. I start to offer him a hand unloading—
he doesn't seem capable of doing it himself—
but I hesitate. I recognize him,
and I don't like being with myself these days.

I hand off my future
and leave it behind me.

My Heart Here Lies

My heart here lies, by my design,
        Open and naked for you to view;
A stronger or truer love than mine
        No other man can show to you!

I wish that I could guarantee
        A restful night, a sleep to renew;
A more peaceful dream than one of me
        No other man can promise you!

Sit at my table—of my dinner partake—
        I'll cook enough food for a restaurant menu;
A tastier meal than the one I bake
        No other man can plan for you!

Laugh at my jokes till your insides quiver—
        I'll not quit till you cry out for mercy, beaucoup;
A funnier line than the one I deliver
        No other man can drop on you!

My music floats lightly like a butterfly on wing—
        Only songs of your love fill my retinue;
A more lyrical poem than the one I sing
        No other man could write for you!

Your warmth in winter (only reside herein)—
        Your coolness in summer—the heat I'll subdue;
A shelter better suited to the change in each season
        No other man would build for you!

My thoughts surround you (a clothing I conceive)—
     From the fringe of your scarf to the heal of your shoe;
A finer raiment than the cloth I weave
     No other man could sew for you!

I'm a life-giving mead (to try and sum up)—
     A magical liquid shared by few;
A drink more quenching than which fills this cup
     No other man can brew for you!

All of my poetry has but one purpose—
     The lines rhyme with you (I see that they do);
The multifarious resonance shared between us
     No other man may pen for you!

Not to Worry

Not to worry!
What I know, I've always known,
And the knowledge didn't stop me
From jumping feet-first back then:
It would not turn my head now.

No need for uneasiness—
If I slipped,
It was because knowing was so familiar to me.
The topic seemed natural and commonplace:
And my only thought was the news would make you happy.

Nothing has changed for me,
Although I know my awareness is fresh for you.
Whatever future confronts us I will be guided
By your wishes and the love of you:
I do not begrudge my relationship with you.

Off-Broadway

The act comes to an end,
and I get up, put my clothes on
and leave.
I thought to myself that the play was dragged out,
that the actors had to convince themselves
that it was worthwhile.
But they had to reach their climax—
(who were driven like me before
themselves).
And I promise I will never again
be dragged down to such cheapness
in action.
I say that I will stay away from the stage
but tomorrow night it will happen—
happen again.
I will return to the theater, glancing
behind my back as I go—maybe
this time they'll catch me.

And now she meets me under the neon lights.
The flashing yellow soon changes to darkened white
and the first act of the night begins.
Tonight there will be three acts
and when the heroine dies, so do I,
and I could kill myself.
Kill myself for once again returning
to the scene of the crime, yet
where else can I go?

The climax comes, I gather my clothes
and leave. The director turns off
the lights.

The city is still flashing yellow outside.
I begin my long walk home, slowly, very slowly,
because I dream of rewriting these plays
that I find always to be the same.
Always to drive deeper and deeper
carrying you along, until you lose
your emotions, and you forget if
the play make sense.
And first you read the critics' reports
and they think and decide you
don't find it as pleasurable
as they did.

But tomorrow night, you realize
will find you stealing from your house,
because it is time.
Time.
Time for the play.
Time for the play to begin,
and wear you down
and drag out your heart
and wear you down, down, down
until you follow
and you can't resist,
and you run through the night thinking of the
lights, and you run all the way until you're
there.
And then you think again (the doors are open)
and stare, and think, and
go in.

On a Journey

This train clanks and hisses along
    And nobody chooses to notice now
        For they've built their backs to my tracks

And then bricked over the windows
    Shuttering me out of their existences
        Except for my underlying angry rumble.

I see their backyards bilious
    With rows of unclipped heightening hedges
        And precocious piles of discarded quiddity

And they won't even read
    The cute sayings and nebulous pictures
        Painted on the sides of my boxcars.

On Page 2

One page 2—people die in neat columns
below their headline grave markers.
Photographs of bodies posed obligingly
with captions explain why they're not moving.
Casualties continue to mount
until on page 7, only maimed
and vegitableized bodies remain.
By page 15 the gore is reduced
to sick and old people.

And then—over leaf—
a poem
by a Pulitzer Prize-winning poet
about a box of fake fruit.

One Raging Year

So one raging, dervish, world-ignoring year,
    and is there still that burning
    red-black coal
    hot enough in our inner selves
    to withstand the nursing home years?
Was it all what we promised it would be
    or can the pundits throw it back in our faces?
Did we overcome the hurdles we knew would be there
    or did we succumb like some TV reality show?

Opposites

I hear the effort in your voice
the ease of our closeness is gone
and its nothing but time and distance.

I can't be allowed out anymore
it's bad for me
I see women
and I compare them to you
and want you.

This is why there should be male-only
Activities
so I don't have to feel the pain.

You could have had us both:
your husband and me
but differently.

Me you could have at your will
and I never asked
but to be ordered about
I need to be owned.

But you wanted to be had by us both:
your husband and me
but differently.

You wanted to be my slave
and have me demand your nakedness
so you could think of the exposure.

Orbit of My Life

I live outside the orbit of my life:
Like a catalyst
I cause the elements around me to jell,
But never become part of the pudding myself.

I leave my life each morning
To become an element in some other catalyst's life,
Where I engage in activities of his choosing,
Performing no functions for my own benefit;
And the fruition of this work
Is passed back
To my life
Where I am not.

At day's end I go back
Tired,
To mingle with tired elements
I sometimes do not recognize,
But who at least have lived
In their own lives that day,
Engaging in actions which revolve around those lives—
Working where they live.

And back in my own life,
Like a hound who's lost the scent,
I'm not always sure
Where I am.

Over Hot, Mellow Tea

Over hot, mellow tea, let us now celebrate together!
I'll read you your tea leaves, and, inspired, reveal then your future:
I'll foretell tranquil days—six months; no, a year; wait, forever . . .
But first let us order: pick whatever is fattening and suits you.

Now then, a toast: To Your Health! (Spiked with cream and sugar) . . .
With those whippoorwill words I'm attempting to convey my joy.
(Why struggle with words—why not just get up and hug her?
Maybe later . . . after my thoughts are expressed—let this rhyme be my
    envoy.)

Have you ever noticed how the sun in summer and winter,
Slowly rises without fanfare, big, and quiet, pale yellow;
How it sucks from the sky all the blue, as if to infer
Its own strength is so great, all others' beauty it can overthrow.

So it is with you—you outshine any other beauty's attempt to compete
By virtue of the strength you have gained in so short a time.
Your smile is radiant with confidence—its reflection bittersweet
In my heart (assuring that I'll always have another mountain to climb).

But in spring and autumn the sun must struggle to shine—
Fighting clouds; damp, hot fogs; cold mists and enveloping rain.
When winning, it bursts forth with a delight it cannot confine,
Spreading orange and gold and rainbows across its domain.

You, too, are this springtime, this autumnal, this sweet-burning sun,
Shaping shadows, casting colors, dancing dew-drops, as you rise higher still.
I'm lovesick—disquieted, left longing, by the splendor of your phenomenon.
Let me soak up your strength—an outstretched tree atop a bare hill.

The poets say spring is rebirth and autumn is dying,
But it's all one life—a continuous, wide-ranging quest.
In my mind spring is for growing and learning—the summer for playing,
Autumn's dance is satisfaction while the winter sings a lullaby of rest.

Right now, two seasons describe you—both springtime and autumn—
You've changed, are still changing and I'm jealous of your freshness and
    youth.
Mixing growth and satisfaction (and knowing them) in soft-swinging
    equilibrium,
As the more you're your own, the better you'll be, in truth.

Once you've quenched your desires, the other two seasons are yours:
First you'll frolic at your control as the Earth Mother in summery full bloom,
And then soon, with the passing of time this perseverance assures
The taking of wintery rest as your rightful bridegroom.

Now I've named you the sun and given you the seasons to boot,
And I've fancied you before as a ship with a brand-new rudder.
So here in my rowboat, my arms aching from fruitless pursuit
I watch you: hauled-in, with my love, as always, your voyageur.

The Pain

Before you . . .
I was a lump of coal:
Dark
Impenetrable

But with the head of love . . .

I am a diamond,
Clear
Sparkling

I can think of no better metaphor.

But with the brightness comes the pain of seeing.
At least before you I was able to keep the longing
buried in the coal bin.

Now it's out for me to see, and the fiery need burns my eyes.

Plad

You came home in the cool evening
with your eye shut tight
smelling of the skunk
who hit you square in the face
filling the house with your presence.

I washed out your eye
but didn't have much luck
washing out the smell.

You were told "you stink"
more than once
as the week went by
and your aroma didn't improve.

And the tomato-juice baths
did nothing but render you pink
with a rash on your back.

Plums

When you were two
we were a constant pair.

I'd carry you on my hip
and we'd sing songs from Sesame Street
and everyone knew us as we
traveled from the butcher
over to the hardware store
out to the vegetable stand
back to the auto parts store
and down to the unemployment office.

Some things I'll never forget:
　　　　how nimbly you'd ride your
　　　　　　　　purple tricycle and Big Wheels;
　　　　the day you called us to witness
　　　　you throwing away your
　　　　　　　　security blanket all on your own;
the time we bought the purple plums.

The sun was high and hot
and we were in the bright green Datsun
running chores.

We stopped at the farm stand
and under the cool awning
I bought broccoli and potatoes
and dark purple plums.

Back in your car seat
I gave you your first-ever plum.

A lover of food,
(my mother and I gave you this gift)
you bit right in
and your eyes burst open with delight.

The cool, sweet juice burst down your face and onto your shirt.
Stupidly concerned for your clothes,
I tried to take the plum away from you.
You fought me for it.

I laughed and let you keep it,
The juice flowed freely and you were quickly
a joyous mess.

I took the pit and
You begged for another
which I gave you;
and,
what the hell,
I had one, too.

We cruised down the tree-lined
street with the hot wind
blowing in the car,
wet, happy and sticky.

Poem with Footnotes

You've asked me so many times:
Why do I love you? So . . .
I'm taking the time
on this rattling, jolting train
to try and write down

My reasons:
>   When I see you:
>>   Joy radiates from your smile[1]
>>>   Like the dawn breaking beneath a sailor's sky.
>>   Your eyes chase, capture and dart away from me
>>>   Causing me to thrash the water madly
>>>>   In my search for the lure.[2]
>>>   Please, cast in my direction one more time!
>>   So smooth—so fair, I see youth, not age:
>>>   The true beauty of a shell isn't complete
>>>>   until the animal inside has passed maturity,
>>>   And as she ages, her shell becomes more beautiful—
>>>>   and so it is with you!

>   When I talk with you[3]
>>   I store every word, hoping to learn more about you—
>>>   There is nothing more interesting to me than you.
>>   Your stories breathe with a humor born of worldliness—
>>>   You've learned to handle the adversary!

---

[1]   You are beautiful when you smile!

[2]   Perhaps I've mentioned that I find you desirable?

[3]   You have a very pleasing voice—clear, unpretentious, crisp.

I can relax in your presence
        And I find myself revealing to your thoughts
                that were never to have passed the boundaries
                of my mind
Reveling in the playground of "intellectual" give and take—
        Your thoughtful perception and quick grasp
        Inspire me to delve further into our relationship.[4]

---

[4]   I guess I'm trying to say you're pretty smart.

Portrait

I have stretched only this one large canvas
and worked it over and over again,
until it sags with paint and age,
with the heavy knife work of depth and hate,
with the fine brush strokes of shadow and love.

Perhaps I should have worked
many smaller canvases,
realizing I could never get the one right.

"I'm not like that," you said,
"don't expect me to splash my colors around."
And I thought this one failing okay.
It never was.

For when I was young I thought myself tough;
I didn't need anyone but me
to mix the colors of my palette.
I never could.

But self-portraits are the toughest,
And no masterpiece this one.
Perhaps if I mount it in a gilded frame
no one will notice.

Portrait in a Restaurant

Smokeless tip
of cigarette glows:
immensity
of storehouse of emotions
within
mirrored
in hungriness of drag.
Physical exertion strains
muscles and cheeks—
reduced to
hollow shadows.
Pulls deep,
V-fingers poised,
surrounding,
until strength of inhalation
wanes.

Cigarette:
suddenly flies
downward in cradle,
arc
of red sky-writing trailing,
to rest on side
on thick rim
of ashtray,
exhaling,
letting off smoke,
relaxing.

Eyes shining deeply,
inset,
in orange glow.
Quickly
snap of tongue
roof of mouth
catches last whiffs
of smoke
attempting to curl
to freedom.

Body upright,
silent:
then blowing
shrinking,
the smoke leaves,
long fluffy
column
ending in confusion.

Now:
cigarette
hand
lips
wait impatiently.

Potmarked

The end of the year
and what have I accomplished in a year?

Although I haven't lived with her for 15 years,
this house, this block was mine
before it was theirs;
A holiday from individuals.

Potmarked like frozen earth after a storm
I sit, waiting for the thaw so the pain will soften.

The Propagation of Brooklynites

                    e e
Once, Darwin—y d,
I witnessed survival of the FITTEST:
The struggle was staged in the grey citiair
amid the dronnnnne of mechanical movers,
in the midst of the machinery OdOr,
A c r o s s the flat blackness
of the roofs of two brown-tiled taxpayers
Joined backtoback,
l
 e
  a
   n
    i
     n
      g
        on each other,
as an old man leans upon his c
                              a
                              n
                              e.

There—
Surrounded by the WaRtS and PiMpLeS
of vents,
Hemmed in by rOlls of tarpaper,
  r   h
t a s
And the signs of defunct businesses
once g   g with the aspirations
        l   n
         o i
          w

of tough, little people—
There an apartment had been built
Above
    one store nearly in the MIDDLE of one side,
One single second story of w
                   i
                   n
                      d o w s

Overlooking the busy
                 boulevard
          below.

The survivors occupying that apartment
in their
           obstreperousness

Had constructed upon this barren soil
          a
      Gar   den
        i   n
       Po   ts

      bright green
   a   plastic
with   awning,

and a white wrought iron

      & table s
        c   r
       h a i
       :

This Garden of Eden
was accessible only
through the BathtuB
              w
              i
              n
                d o w.

Radical

I seem to have become a radical
all over again.
Why can't I find a woman
at peace enough with herself
that she can forsake
the gaudy displays
of wealth (to whatever extent
she can pull it off to begin with);
of power (to whatever extent
she can bully people);
of sex (the most important,
most forced guideline of all).

Rainy Day

Once I left my daughter standing in the rain.
Though I blame myself
It wasn't just me.
It could have been my wife;
It could have been the babysitter.

The neighbors drove by but she wouldn't get in the car.

Today she reminds me
that I didn't bring her up;
she grew up herself

as she struggles to make her checkbook balance
or figures how to fix her car.
And I think maybe I didn't do so badly after all.

The Reader

The MC calls for order,
apologetically.
Some have been waiting and quickly become
attentive.
Others have been busy listening to themselves
chatting.
The applause is noncommittal,
questioning.

In the quiet

                        attentiveness

she works her way

                through the tables

                            to the stage.

Arranging her water and notebook
she appears too slight for the magnitude of the occasion,
yet she has already stolen our silence for her own.
If at this moment,
she were to look up and fix us with just the intensity of her thoughts
and leave,
we would remain, pondering.

But she begins,
and the force of her words rattle the preconceptions loose
and
     they
         fall
and
     c r u m b l e.

The lessons she's teaching aren't timid;
they don't hide behind innuendo.
She questions the relationships:
          father/daughter,
          principal/servant,
          user/lover.
She tells of her pain in each
                              and of how she survived.

She searches the audience
to find those who need to have the words driven home;
her eyes fix them.
She leans into us, watching,
and urges the words upon us.
Can we do any less than she with our own petty lives?

I take my own accusations from the stories.
Would I want to take this beauty as they had,
or be taken by her? Could I just adore her?
But I don't know if as a temple or flesh.
I'm precluded anyway, which is best.

And she's not afraid of her own poems
although she should be.
They're powerful—
they should scare the audience away, too.
My maleness feels
like standing naked before her.
I cannot separate myself from my brothers.
I wonder if I should leave.

She weaves the patchwork quilt of her life for us.
We follow her down the weaving path,
mixing metaphors, as life does.
She's still searching, even as she leads us.
I gaze with her into the forest,
and try to separate the shadows from the real.
My eyes aren't that good.

She closes with love,
and there's fire here, too.
It's her personal metaphor,
glowing red in her hair, her eyes, her twang.
She's a lot for me to learn.

Religion

I've decided to start my own religion
and I've based it on lack of worship
In my religion there will be no worship of a god
no worship of a founder
no worship of certain principles
or of nature, animals or man

My religion should have no group sufferers,
only personal suffering
Each person shall be spared
the compassion of the others

Solitary suffering is best

S.

What made her decide she was finishing living?
Finished feeling, finished revealing, had started dying?

I've never cared who died leaving monuments behind—
I can walk around a monument and be done with it.

I've never cared who died leaving nothing but air behind them—
I can sanitize, sweep, with white apron, and be done with them.

But to cut my chest with so huge, so sharp a knife;
To leave my guts hanging red, bloody, dripping, clotting, brown;

To scrawl doubts, like subway graffiti across
The tiled walls of my cavernous mind;

And then to disappear with the bandages and disinfectant
Locked tight in the vacuum of her mouth . . .

Numb thoughts—where the trail ends and the forest begins,
After having walked, strode, trotted, galloped with hers,

Open-mouthed, hot, panting—beat the inside walls of my skull
Like a child locked forever inside a discarded refrigerator.

It's the might-have-been, should-have-been, could-have-been
That haunts and chants and shutters inside my throbbing head.

Is there a piece of her left? Are all the fragments swept up?
Would the next poem have been the one to set me at peace?

She's cheated me, though she owed me nothing,
But is there like the dust-clean outline of her book.

She had no right to become part of my life
After she was dead, was dead, was dead.

Safety Check

I'm okay . . .
> if I don't think about
>> the smooth silk that is a woman's
>> skin.
> if I don't remember
>> how naturally I slide into the groove
>> of her back,
>> the firm mound of her rump.
> when I don't miss
>> her musk soaking my beard,
>> the aroma accompanying only me
>> as I go about my daily business.

I'm okay . . .
> if I don't think about you.

But in the absence of your wink
and Want-it? swish of your hips
a solo piano fills my head with blues so deep
I feel exhausted just expending the effort to listen to it,
and there's nothing left for me to do
> but shut down my systems again.

I put my hard(hat) on for protection
and walk the aisles,
cleaning out the bins.

I find the sultry glance you gave me over your shoulder:
I categorize and file it.
I review the meeting you flashed your legs at me from welcome to gavel;
I seal those minutes shut and lock them.

As I throw each toggle
                      in the prescribed order
it snaps solidly (I pray) off
until at last it's safe to kill the master switch.

The turbo is silent;
Let's hope no one else flips it on again.

The Sea before The Storm

I need no help from the woman on the Weather Channel
with the 60's-like psychedelic wall
to know a nor'easter is coming.
The warm, mouth-filling wind howls down
from Boston, bringing what feels like my youth
rattling among the bare tree branches.
I decide I must visit this winter beach,
and so I clean up the kitchen, and leave.

I always bring too thin a coat,
but the chill from the sea feels cleansing
once my body settles down to its new temperature.
I hold the car door for the dog a moment,
and then remember he's not with me.
I feel remiss that his nose won't play over this wind.

I walk the first muddy cove,
past the jetty, and onto the beach,
but the news is not much
more enlightening than standing in my kitchen
pulling fat from inside the Christmas goose;
if a storm is coming,
the cove is stoically unconcerned,
as if it is content that this man-made beach
will now receive its just punishment.
I've seen the same calm in some women's eyes
as they glance over at their husbands at parties.

I reach the head of the neck
and begin the climb up the rocks
to the highest, most seaward point.
The wind now chooses to remind me of
who it is who owns the sea
(you may ask any sailor)

and begins to hurry me from behind.
My clothes are pressed smooth behind me,
but in the front the loose cloth gathers
at my biceps and shins
wiggling like a worm first exposed to the sun.
Is it only humans that prefer the wind to their backs?

I work my way over the rocks,
choosing my footfalls among the sea-lined boulders.
Sometimes I choose the tanned, lined rocks above the water line,
and sometimes I dip down to their black-stained companions below
to be close to the water.
There are no gusts to throw me off-balance,
just this constant presence from the north.
If I'm momentarily off-balance it's my own fault
for not compensating for the pressure.
So it is everywhere, I think dryly,
pursing my lips, nodding my head
and snorting in agreement.

Eventually, I stand directly above the sea
and the wind howls at my defiance.

The sky is a ceiling of gull-grey clouds
like the long-forgotten insulation in god's attic
turned upside down.
It is unbroken
from here to Long Island
where three smokestacks hold their corner taut.

The colorless sea is contained.
It sports no white-caps; it flashes
no underbellies of green color. It is fermenting;
its intensity is below. It rolls and chops
a little, looking like the frosting of an army-ordered cake.
Perhaps it will explode; perhaps
it's only a dud.

I move down the cliff
and the wind abruptly stops pushing me.
Squatting down on my haunches
not far from the water, I watch it lap over the now-bare rocks.
I've stood on those same rocks at low tide
and cast for fish. They were slippery with algae then,
and had I caught a fish,
we both might have had to swim for it.
Small compensation, to be dry.

I wonder where the birds have gone;
they are neither floating on the water
nor huddling on the beach.
I look in the leeward cove for them,
where it is amazingly calm
for all the confusion to windward,
but they're not there either.
The sea, bored with such mundane observations,
splashes me to move me along. I take my host's point
(having expected more of me after so many visits)
and climb back up and continue down
the far side of the neck.

Here the sea gives itself away; it knows.
The water excitedly rushes out the channel
from the pond behind, eagerly joining the
dance in the Sound. Tonight it will rumble.
I decide to return tomorrow.

The Sea after The Storm

I work my way to the beach in the early
morning dampness. If it were summer, this
would be fog. Today it's just another element of the cold.
I weave between severed limbs,
and detour around downed trees. I wonder
at the detached branches held up by their healthier
brothers, and for what purpose. I look for allegory.

When I arrive at the beach,
the sea is raging. Now the whitecaps jump and
fret like spoiled children.
Now the waves
try to use the confusion on the surface
to mask their approach,
but the swelling gives them away.
They begin their assault
within sight of the shore,
rising up with the roar of a war-cry,
and rumbling up the sand,
but then hissing as they fall back
defeated. The beach just has too many foot-grains
to throw into the fray.

I look for the high tide line from
last night's storm—its jumble of
Spartina, shells (both mollusk and shotgun),
frayed lobster pot lines and sliced
foam buoys of Crayola colors,
plastic bottle and Tampax applicators—
but the shore is clean
except for the occasional large cluster
of oysters and their knuckles
half buried in the wet, grey sand.

This is odd.

The beach is different in a more subtle way, too.
Red sand streaks the tan
as if the land had burst a vein
in the battle last night.

A little further along the cove
and I see that my sea
has been the victor once more.
The sea wall has been breached
during the night.
An inland sea now exists, where once
there was grass and a path and
picnic tables.

The gulls—reappeared as a multitude—
cover this new body of water,
feeding on the salt-surprised
worms and grubs
who thought early enough to escape their water-filling
burrows. So much for the theory
of survival of the most intelligent.

I climb the freshly laid sand ramp to the top of the wall,
and the gulls rise in disgust,
as white-gowned protestant ladies
undoubtedly would at the sight
of my haphazard Sunday dress and grooming.
Their leaving uncovers the white line separating the
bicycle/rollerblading path
from the walking/jogging path
beneath the flood. The fish and starfish
choose not to obey the lines. They have
little to lose at this point.

The gulls cry out to emphasize they are
awaiting my departure. They make only slight
angling adjustments,
tacking against the still-strong wind
to maintain their vantage above me.
Reminded that gulls only shit over
solid objects (of which there are
not many left on the beach, save me)
I resume my journey.

As I approach the brackish pond that
intermarries with the ocean here (sharing their children
with each high tide),
I see, unbelievably,
two windsurfers. They struggle to right their sails,
but can only hold them up for a moment
before succumbing to the strength
of the wind. The sail and surfer go in opposite directions.
The only progress they achieve is
to edge slowly closer and closer
to the weir
that separates the pond from the ocean.
The tide is abnormally high, though, so
the only danger is bruised legs and skegs.
I leave them to their own brand of folly
and return to mine.

As I near the last leg of my circum-walk
the wind begins to drive a fresh rain
and I find a set of keys. There are keys to
four automobiles, an electronic alarm
button for a Saab, and two house keys,
one the old-fashioned kind the jailer
in the cowboy moves always had
on a big ring. There is no fob. I

immediately conclude the man
who lost these keys
would have his Saab with him.
Since the parking lot is within sight,
and newly hooded figures are leaning
in that direction, I take the keys
with me and head that way, too.

There is no Saab or Subaru. There is
one Chrysler. There are several Fords. I opt
for the Chrysler and park near it.
Shortly, a woman approaches the Chrysler,
warily eyeing me
in my beard, in my slick, in my truck
and quickly opens and locks the door of
her car and leaves. I eye the Fords, but
soon their owners come and leave. Within
half an hour I am the only car left in the
parking lot. One of his children must
have delivered another set of keys. I leave.
I take the keys with me.

Back at home the old fashioned key fits my bedroom door.
I look for my jailer
to tell her she has lost her keys.

Shade Tree

If I take my means of life
into my hands
and with prickly smell pawn it off
on this one or that one,
will this life become the child
of quicker streets
or will I carry my freedom in a lunch pail
or surround myself by brick walls?

Dare I
carve circles around beauty
and watch as its sap runs out?
And if my child
of quicker streets
were my sapping beauty . . .

I love my passion,
I can create and murder
in one act.

If you take my means of life
into your hands
and hold it,
will not this life become the child
of beauty,
whose shades will comfort,
whose sap will not run
but to another?

Side-tracked

Don't candle me:
I might not be fertile—
Don't p a   d my c
        e   r   n   o
        e ou   rner:
            k
Façade & 2x4s may be all i am—
Don't crack this royal blue, gold-tooled binding;
My story may be drug-store sterile.

You've mistaken me;
        piece
I'm meal—not Whole—
Having been t   s   e   together over the years,
            o s d
Like a bumper covered with once-true stickers,
Or a great stockyard,
Where my
Beliefs, thoughts and ideas
Roam the rails of my mind
Seeking a way out.

Sentences—
H-i-t-c-h-e-d together loaded boxcars—
Search for a caboose,
(Every sentence must have a caboose)
And very often,
In their hurry,
H-i-t-c-h up empty cars—
Not realizing the mistake until
After the train has already left the yard,
When strangers stare
At the train r u s h i n g by
Pulling some boxcars whose doors gape hOllOwly.

All the while FULL boxcars
Are left rusting speechless in the yard,
Ideas locked,
Slammed tight
Within—and some others, the contents
Too hastily sorted and closed,
Are prone to s

       p
         i

            ll their cargo before their
Final destination.

As now,
A train ro
      ck
      in
      g
Precariously from s   s
             i to i
             d   d
             e   e
G o e s   w h i z z i n g   t h r o u g h
with phrase
upon
phrase
Coupled together, and exits,
WhiStle blowing,
From the tunnel of my mouth.
(And you've sworn to me often enough, Love
That this tunnel
Is one of the busiest you've ever known
Even when the engines
Are only moving empty boxcars.)

LOOk a   d:
          r   n
            ou
Rust-covered raIls double—to unused
                point—
        Regions of knowledge,
Once   labored, but long since laid fallow,
     heavily
          Where t scraggly, s
                a   k
                l   i
                l weeds   n
                ,   n
                           y
        With bright blooming purple buds
              STAND
              Defiantly
        Between the tic   toe of   and
                  —tac—   ties   raIls
            p   mowed
        To be icked or down
          Some ha lf
        And some full bloomed:
              Unplanned,
              Not planted.

        Along other right-of-ways
          The under premises
               lying
          Are rott e n . . .
        Where too many have succumbed
        The raIls have been thr
                        o
                          w
                            n

And a percepTION lies on its s

                          i

                          d

                          e,

The only parts still shiNNy

Being the bo   oms of its once spinning

          tt

Metal wh e e ls—

(She had s p e e d, if nOthing else.)

But in the mid.dle

Of the yard,

One track

                    rn

With many switches and tu o

                      f

                      fs

Is covered,

Except for the top shiNing surface of the raIls,

With a thick blanket of smoke,

Settled

To form a SOLID mass

Of gravel, smoke and ties:

So firm a footing

That through trains

Often ignore the speed limit!

I hope those tracks must never be revised.

Tools of the trade—

Thrown aside rustily upon the grass

Unperceived,

Unperceiving,

No perception:

(Did I miss something? Did I blow it again?

Why am I told

I'm forever wrong

When I'm doing the best I can?

Lying here,

Bleedin   orange.)

    g

ching
The swit   stations
Are kept mopped, but not dusted—
Some are clean;
Where machines live,
Those 10 foot tall mathematicians
l   c i   g   s a p n , c u   t   n
With c i   k n ,   n p i g   o n i   g
Fingers
Covering their chests and stomachs.
(Had I so many levers and toes
I might count too!)
But the raIls
Surrounding
Are rusty from signals
Unflashing for too long,
Despite the seats of learning within—
Beer cans and cobwebs.

I have chosen to hide
beside
Power lines   the grade,
Pipes and wire   the gravel,
beneath
And to stockpile ties, spikes, raIls
In empty parking lots
Near silent repair sheds.

So leave me
In the dark,
Where my color will not pale;
In the bottle,
Where my fragrance will not be found flat;
In the sheath,
Where my blade will not be tested.

Kept locked
In the back of your drawer
Unused
I'll always be available
In an emergency
Even if useless
Like a life preserver
Made of bricks.

Sighing

Now sighing has become a rather large part of my life,
When speechless we two sigh as the next best means to communicate;
Your longing, sad sigh sharply cuts me through like a knife,
To which I respond with a sigh to tell you I'm frustrated.
I'd fill your body with my own if only I could,
Close the gaps in your physic and trade your skin for my skin;
But I vowed I'd not do it long ago, and my vow is still good,
And the keeping of it at your sight is no mean discipline.
The holes in the speeches I deliver are filled with my sighs,
They represent the words too difficult to mouth on their own;
I listen and your sigh in response to mine than replies,
You know what I'm thinking for I can tell by your tone.
> We've a communication more meaningful than the English
> language we speak,
> By sighing our souls converse and find the fulfillment they seek!

Smiles

Yesterday
you looked up at me
sad, burdened by the work you had yet to do
and tried to put me off.

But I was patient and waited
and when you were done (though late)
we rendezvoused . . .
                    and broke away at last.

And the sun shone on your face,
the worries began to smooth away
until finally
              you smiled

and then so did I.

Sound Bites

I

All that is required
for a seagull game of
follow-the-leader
is one morsel of food
a little too big for one swallow.

II

Is your skin
smooth and silky?
I dream it is.

III

telling stories on the telephone
tantalizing
listening for breathing
touching myself and pretending it's you

IV

See yourself
        for what you are,
and not for what others
        would have you be.

V

I should find it easy to write about you,
    I have so much to tell.
But your power is such the words fail me
    Miserably.

I search for a single word
that won't wither before
I can bring it to you . . .

Magnificent?

How can it be that both you and English
leave me with an unfulfilled need?

VI

I see you . . .

Work your own way through your problems
confidently, in control

It was nothing new that others hadn't done before
hiding behind work.

VII

The eyes tighten and pierce
then widen and sparkle:
The tease starts down deep.

VIII

I think of you and
        I smile . . .
I want you and
        My body warms.

IX

A gentleness blankets my world
        when you walk through my mind . . .
A meteorite craters my chest
        when you race through my bloodstream.

X

The everyday parking lot on a warm spring night.
Sounds of basketball:
                        Shut them out.
And there's us
                And a promise
I have no trouble asking
But I forever will trouble not to forget.

XI

The reality of you
        is more brilliant than the dream.

XII

Beauty isn't enough
        Although it's plain to see in you.
Laughter isn't enough
        Although it's here; it hides behind each move.

XIII

The strut exudes sex
I've seen the look in other men's faces:
No admiring glances here,
                              just longing ones.
They see the Adventure in that quick, knowing smile.

XIV

I am not mine.
You must plant your flag here.
What right would I have to want you
If you do not make me yours?

XV

A confused rush and tumble of feelings.
I cannot sort them!
More input than I've needed to field in years:
I am out of practice.

XVI

Standing in your lair,
          kneeling at your feet,
                    scarred by your pleasure
                              bound in your love.

XVII

If you own me, prove it.
Toy with my mind, my body:
Leave me in pain at your whim.
If it amuses you . . .
                    take my weakness
                                        in your hands
and squeeze and pull
until the pain is the fulfillment of desire.
I succumb.

XVIII

You're not here, yet you interrupt my work
out of nowhere.
The cadence of your voice
fills and distracts me
and I pause;
letting the laughter of your full
smile baste me
in my heat.

XIX

Here I am outside your world
carving a place for myself.
Trying to burrow in like a cat
seeking your warmth in the winter.
And I'm eager to be a prostitute to you,
to be yours in any way I can,
As long as I'm yours.

XX

Deny me
            because I've been cold so long.
I need the warmth of longing to kindle in me again
the desire I haven't felt since I was younger.
Stoke me,
            please.

XXI

The problem is . . .
To first find my voice,
And then,
Having found it
To relate the story . . .

XXII

Like a lily waking to the warmth of the morning sun
Love opens you up
And there's always more
    Love,
    Sunshine,
    Possibilities,
When you're open to accept the outpouring.

The Space Between Our Touchings

The space between
our touchings
is a void I must fill
with work,
memories of you
and this poem.

This poem is a flower,
and although offered
by a ragged peddler of poetry,
it is not frivolous—
the petals of this flower
do not repeat "he loves me . . .
he loves me not":
it is a hybrid, this flower,
it has taken a long time
to grow.

Pluck a petal:
My first wish is—
            May your day be filled
            with the smiles
            of 2600 happy
            out-of-towners!
Pluck another:
            May your room
            have an instant-on TV set,
            whose picture isn't just
            blotches of red and blue

And another:
> May you sleep
> undisturbed and arise
> fully rested each morning

For this flower is for you.
> . . . to pluck a petal to read
>> each night while you're away;
> . . . to bloom and smile
>> and keep you company
>> while I cannot;
> . . . to fill the need in me
>> to tell you:

I love you!
I pause each day
to smile
as my mind turns
to you,
and I devote hours
to remembering
> your sweet voice,
> and the words we've shared
>> your quips,
>>> followed by that wide, gentle smile
>> your beauty
>>> which is great.

I miss you
> . . . and the madness
>> excitement and
>> confusion of the show;
> . . . the stuffing and
>> restuffing of thc file folder;
> . . . tea for four
>> for two.

So keep this flower
well-watered
until we are united again.
Place it where these bright colors
can be easily seen—
Where it can dispel
any gloom attempting
to enter your life.

Starting from Scratch

Not to be outdone
by the sidewalk peddlers
hawking their wares
on every downtown corner,

This bum has set up shop
in the alley, in front of
his favorite heating exhaust vent.

The corner bookstore
had thrown out
a carton of dime-store romances
, sans covers,
and returned them for credit
safe in the warning to consumers
not to buy books without covers.

Greatcoat
discovered them rummaging
through the Dempster dumpster.

So he huddles
on the cement
with his back to the grate
adding his molding presence
to the already heavy
smell of the humid exhaust
with the faceless books

each hidden behind the mask
of the publisher's serial promo,
stacked on the overturned carton
between him and the few
passers-by by-and-large.

Greatcoat is sleeping.
No one thumbs the books.

Sounds of barter
on adjourning streets
occasionally rise
above the noise of
the city in motion.

Stranger

This woman lies asleep next to me
More familiar to me than I am to myself,
And, after all these years,
As bland as boiled chicken on Thursday.

Every habit, every motion,
Every topic of discussion
And every opinion
Haunts like a ghost from the past—
The predictability is what defeats me.

I know the answer to the question even as I ask.
I know the reaction to the problem even as it unfolds.
And I can follow the pattern which proceeds
        The slump into a timeworn habit.
The colloquialisms, the habitualisms, the mannerisms
        Do not irritate me—
It is knowing that they will occur next
        That infuriates me.

Saturday holds no surprises
So why shouldn't I wake up foul?

And the other side of the coin—
This person who I know so well
Knows me not at all . . .

I guess I gave up long ago
When I failed to see any light of understanding
        Beginning to dawn in those hardened eyes.
And so I receded before the selfishness
        That increases and increases the longer we are together.

She seldom catches my moods.
If I want quiet, loving sex
I am met with noisy exuberance.
When I need reassurance I am handed more insecurity.
When I need to be selfish even more is demanded of me.

So I have built a space between us
And with each denial or new demand
I widen the ditch between us by
Another spadefull of dirt.

Surely you can't expect me to fill in in a day
A ditch that has taken years to dig?

Surgery

The patient is due for surgery once more
The surgeons stand around her in their green uniforms
and with their sharp instruments cut the already
many-times scared body
that has been operated on enough times
it resembles a dried riverbed
open once again

The backhoes tear her skin away
and push aside the underlying muscle
to reveal the damaged veins below

With the ease of experience, the damaged vein
is replaced and the clamp removed to let the muscle
fall back into place

They suture her cut and leave

Another scar to slowly heal

Thirty-one

A springwell of emotions within me
Surges against the dam of self-restraint I've built
Whenever you smile.

And then, all my wants assault my mind!
I want! I want!
> To explore every inch of you with my mouth;
>> tasting with my tongue,
>> inhaling your scent.
> To take you into my mind;
>> show you who I am,
>> give you all I possess.
> To share a moment of love;
>> smiling with our knowledge,
>> touching ever so gently.

> Alone.

And this I need more than want—
A time you can spare for me.
When the world will form a void around us,
For then my strength and love are renewed.

You can give me little more than this . . .
> And little more than this can I take!

This Involuntary Twitch

This involuntary twitch as you fall off to sleep
What can it possibly mean, love?
You shouldn't jump while in my arms
Nor dream an unhappy dream, love.

As you slept your hand flinched twice
While resting on my chest, love
"No" I heard, but then you mumbled—
I could not catch the rest, love.

I'd relinquish my happiness to gain the power
Your worries to erase, love
To never see another frown
Pass across your face, love.

This Page

This page has had the better of me.
I was dry, I had lost my harmony,
Had lost my iambs, lost my meter,
And my choice of rhymes could have been neater.
The vocabulary on the tip of my tongue,
Was not what you'd call very far-flung.

But then I heard your voice, my love,
It woke my conscious, gave me the shove
I needed to resolve once more to write,
Because my work gives you delight.

The sound, so soft, so smooth, so pleasing,
Of your voice, is to me both refreshing and teasing:
While it fills me with joy it also requires
I work on my verses to fill your desires.

I struggle with each work, because I wish to always be
Near, at your hand, your most wide-eyed devotee.
And I know it would not be so hard to write
If I were merely to sit down and recite
The very first thoughts that come to my mind
But then I'd no right to have them enshrined
By your kind, gentle hands, for they wouldn't be worthy
Of you. So I choose my words carefully
And think of witty jokes to make
Which will make this poem a keepsake
With perfect rhymes and a beat that's true
Only then will this poem by good enough for you,
My love.

Through a Hallway Buzzer

"Whom shall I say is calling . . . ?"

Tell her it is I:
     The man with more words
          than tongues to mouth them;
     The boy with more dreams
          than nights to hope them;
     The guardian whose metal visor
          is only painted cardboard.

Tell her it's the one who:
     Stopped taking life as a joke
          but never learned to be serious;
     Seldom seems to know any better
          and, if and when, is always forgetting;
     Follows her from room to room
          to lay at her feet once there.

And who tries to be:
     The crispness of a young year's morning
          filled with the smell of fresh-mowed grass;
     An exotic, aromatic, ice-cold tossed salad,
          with a never-ending variety of vegetables and fruits;
     The sweetness of hot chocolate
          at the foot of a snow-covered mountain.

But who only is:
     A plastic replacement part
          where the OEM was stainless steel;
     The eye of the storm
          which is surrounded by destruction;
     A barnyard strutter
          who only performs when the pen is empty.

For I am:
>He who is inscribed with her name
>>deeply etched in the silverplate of my base;
>He who, when she had won first place,
>>was given her to hold for only a moment;
>He who is locked away in a glass trophy case
>>where she can read her name but never touch.

Tell her . . . it's only me:
>>She'll recognize the name.

Time and Again

Time and again
your tantalizing, gentle voice calls to me
through the copper wires,
over the unseen airwaves,
down the high-tech fiber optics.

My day circles around your call.
I smile.
I try to make you laugh,
and when I do,
I feel the heat of your eyes twinkling
at the other end of the line.

The space between our talks
is a void I fill with work and chores,
memories of you,
and poems that I spend hours
trying to coax to glamour,
yet they always end up
as crumpled scrapes of written-over paper.

I touch you more often than just the few
infrequent moments we spend together.

Time, Gentlemen

Each man marks the morrow's sun rise
when Time arrayed in pen strokes,
when Time will trumpet
the world to the body—
grown food to shoven dirt:
will trumpet rats wrapped in pen strokes
with squeaking claws
upon the streets.

The sweet smelling fog floats burning
around the eyes,
the light's rite
and long-tailed story
ambush the velvet-windowed dead.
How soon My plague?

Old woman bent black,
dismisses a walking shroud,
but the sky in love
burns and marries red and yellow.
Eyes (heavy below—acid above)
follow the target.

Yet butterfly gaily dances before the devil eye
into the fragrant hothouse
fog. The black-ribbed dog pants
his eyes white, pants his body hidden—
hidden in this akin, grim, sea of hymn and sin.

To:

(Disguised as a Poem)

At first:
       the fascination was with beauty and laughter.
Then were revealed:
       traces of myself—fears, thought, doubts,
                        in HER!
Now a yearning, and when my affection was returned:
                         LOVE!

Adolescent, heart-beat-skipping   LOVE!

I wanted to know more—
              to know *everything*;
To be the Only One, the Protector, the Friend;
Hold tenderly!
       Guard in peaceful sleep!
                Kiss!
                   Touch!
                      Squeeze!

But months passed and before I felt I was strong enough
       to lay bare the fabric of my thoughts (Love),
       lay the nets upon the beach in full sunlight,
           To either dry and become brittle,
           Or to soak up strength for deeper trawls through my mind.

All that could be offered, was:
        Love, Friendship, the knowledge that I
                would always be in the back of Her mind,
                                        standing there
and Smiling,
            saying:
"Let me make your life a little happier by my existence;
        Remember that I'll love you . . . always!"

You see: the world had imprisoned my mind with propaganda
            designed to hold me back—and it was working!
Unable (because of them) to be little more than an adoring
                                        puppy,
My Love was so strong that I was satisfied with this role:
If I could make her happy by wagging my tail
        then that would be more than enough!

To an Ideal

You are as elusive
As a speck of dust
Dancing in the fluid
Of my searching eye:

You are on the periphery
Of my vision, but if I
Focus in an effort to see
You straightaway,

All I catch
Is a fleeting glimpse
Of a mischievous you
Quickly dodging away,

Leaving me to wonder
For an instant; until,
Made of gossamer,
You slowly edge back

At my gazing away
As I try to be noncommittal
And to hide my dismay
At having lost you again.

The Trip

Jumping up from the bed naked
      in our cramped hotel room,
you stare back at me for reassurance
      in your presumed wantonness,
thrilling at the appreciation in my eyes.

Unashamedly you pause to give me time to look you over
      as an artist might his just-sculptured beauty,
lean, long, firm—even your fingers and toes long and exquisite,
      the forming bruises where you bumped into the open cabinet door
Imperfections that only increase my curiosity.

I gaze at your hard nipples,
      the slight roundness of your stomach.
I linger at your pubic hair, enjoying
      the added height it gives your virginal mound.
I cannot help but smile, you move on, warmed.

We go to dinner in a large, empty room full of diners
      whose walls are doors open to the night.
The harpist plucks a back-of-the-mind melody,
      the individual notes drifting to us on the breeze
as we memorize each other's movements.

The wine steward tells us what he pours
      with each new architecturally correct course
and we laugh at his detailed pretentiousness
      as we drink the good wine
and soak in our own brewing juices.

We go sightseeing in the morning—
      mountain ranges importantly named,
dead people's homes and purposeful exhibits—
      but the sights are ordinary and I tire of them;
I steal hugs in quiet moments.

Exchanging glimpses through cluttered, dusty
      racks of what passes for antiques,
I bend to examine one,
      but forget which drew me down
I'm so conscious of being close to your skin.

The drives between are long and irrelevant
      as we talk, touch and tease.
You don't flower so much as burst open,
      your pent-up feelings flying out, searching for a nesting ground.
The highway signs come and go with precision,
      as what we've become pleasantly meanders in new directions.

Two Lives

It'd taken nearly two hours of connecting subways
to get back to see him.
But he didn't look like himself, as they say.
They'd soothed out the lines
and taken away the worries
that gave him his character.
I knelt and closed another chapter.
I didn't know the family,
but they knew my name.
I left.

On the way home
I traded a subway token for a paper and change,
because the woman couldn't break a twenty
that late at night.
The kids on the subway
cavorted and strutted as they always have.
Brooklyn hadn't changed
even if two lives had.

The Two of You

The longer, the more closely
I study this spiraled shell,
The more beautiful, the more fascinating
I realize her to be.

As the life within daily
Struggles for (survival and) sometimes pleasure,
Each day it succeeds
                        enhances the splendor
Of this ever-growing home.

No one else rewards themselves
So highly for the achievement of sundown:
A toughening of her skin
                        (a challenge to her opponents);
An increase in her elegance (more deadly than any predator).

More flutes, more whorls,
A heightening and deepening of color
(rich royal purple
                     and silvery mother of pearl);
Polished to a luster, a quiet glow.

What other form of living
Ages so magnificently or
Is lovelier with each new hour?
                        I can think of not one,
Except for you, Love.

U Killed My Cat

On the night-darkened, moon-mellowed tire-resonant roadway
a clandestine mourner has yelled in coldly,
carefully lettered, white spray paint:

       U KILLED
       MY CAT
       U ASS
        NOW
       I HOPE
         U
        DIE
        DIE
        DIE

I've read this open-mouthed hatred for the last three weeks as I've jogged by,
huffing, feet pounding in my ears, mind-churning.
But sometime yesterday the town maintenance crew—
orange-vested and protected by blinking yellow-arrowed lights
and orange cones tabby never had—
tried to obliterate the memorial
(perhaps remembering their own thumping roadside kills)
with shiny black paint
(no one caring enough to consult on the match to the worn tarmac).
The wide-eyed, back-arched, stretching blood and fur
and smell of fear are gone,
but the reverberating words are etched,
screaming, racing for the woods,
in my mind:
DIE, DIE, DIE.

Further down the road—
when my pace-induced breathing has leveled out—
a roadside memorial to a high school student
has been assembled
around the squat, sturdy, thick tree—
buttressed by an old New England-fitted stone wall—
where he killed himself more than a month ago,
accelerating from the tempting red light
at the multi-intersection intersection.
Rotted cut-flowers,
still wrapped in easily-bought stapled plastic.
A potted plant in a facsimile plastic clay pot,
now dead—just limbs, too.
A blue football jersey,
arms hugging the tree,
longing to slide slowly to the ground,
with magic-markered good-byes.
Tearful letters in sheet protectors,
their illegibility further assured by the rain.
And, strangely, a hinged Hallmark "HAPPY."
The shoulder is littered with shattered plastic pieces of car,
(that I dance around,
protecting my ankles),
that no one seems ready to tidy up.
I eye this once-again mess he's left behind him
(there are others on the road,
whose telltale shards increasingly disappear daily)
and just keep pumping
through my arms, legs, lungs and mind.

The stripped lines and segments of pavement
pass underfoot one by one in numbered relentless rhythm
—three steps from start to finish.
(Step on a crack, break your mother's back.)
Death does not ride restless over my shifting shoulders
nor grin in the glaring, gleaming headlights.
I cannot question—nor care to rationalize about—
the apparent appropriateness of each echoing ending.
Two lover raccoons somehow struggle awkwardly, safely,
untabby-like,
across the road and down a sewer.
A skunk, in its naiveté, defies both flesh and machinery.
A buck has learned to ignore the relentless resonance of tires,
but heeds the irregular pounding of feet
as I slow to pray to him.

Tonight I attend a wake and stare cold-hearted
and cold-eyed
at the priest who intones ancient written words
he takes silly solace in,
but doesn't understand.

I wonder if, behind their lens,
his eyes have turned cats-eyes.

Upon Building a Dream

A man,
A century ago,
Proudly
Engraved his name
and the date
on this now-decrepit old Brooklyn brownstone.

When did dreams,
Cast in Concrete,
become so fragile?

Who
will dream this dream again?

We Said It Would Be Different

We said it would be different after we were merrily married,
but it's different only in the twice-seen reflection of our everyday lives;
we were, before we lived it, before we shouldered it.
We're sadly, tip-toey tentative at times in our new related roles,
although the otherwise bellwether change shaped us long before the day
we stood in the dry breeze, under the vigilant sun, above the quiet old river,
with easeful hawks as our witnesses;
a day that had a defining purpose
not for us, but for those who,
with squinted, quizzical eyes,
questioned us.

The broad, unmeasured plains lay before us,
as we trot from different compass points to an ill-determined juncture,
our speed and apex determined not by us,
but by our hired mounts,
who know only the speed of those who rode similarly before us.
with banners unfurled, glinting in the sun.

Between is the practical; the need to eat,
sleep, clean, and attend to the mouths of need
that beseech us.

We Were Conferring

We were conferring by telephone.
We had just wrapped up the details
I was assembling my documents
when you mentioned
      you and your lover
         were calling
            it quits.

So I sat down to listen
But you said it was okay;

And we both had commitments.

Weekends

Can I describe what seeing you today will do to me?
I will want you all weekend
   Remembering the faces you pulled
   the suggestion of your breasts
   your voice, your legs

   The hunger will grow
   so I will crave you all the more
   on Monday

   Each trite love song the radio plays
   will take on meaning

   I will write a poem
   to find a way to talk to you
   if only in my head

   I will be torn
   between the joy of remembering
   the few moments we were together
   and the sadness of remembering
   the few moments we were together

It's happened before
Can it be enough for you to know I love you?

When I Think of You

When I think of you, standing here on the dock, I think . . .
How can I help make her voyage a smooth one?
Is there any way I can influence the gods
To look over her shoulder and fill her sails with their breaths?
                    And I worry . . .

Should I encourage her to take the helm alone?
        Do I have the right to influence her?
Should I suggest she smash her compass and follow the stars
        Or am I out of line?

She's safe in the harbor now, although the waters
        beneath her keel are shallow;
If she puts out to sea, where the waters are deep,
        what safety will she have with her port of call
            still beyond the horizon?

I watch as each day the ship is being prepared for voyage
and yet—the pleasures of the harbor only await discovery.
She has the ability to withstand a storm,
        although the navigator is new to her job, and
        needs to build up her confidence.

The navigator stands over her charts—
        setting her course based
                on the voyages of those before her,
As some day others will follow her voyage for inspiration—
        If she only knew that!

And . . . still standing on the dock
    I beg her—stay in the harbor
        As I have always known you—
    Your graceful lines more beautiful than any
        other ship at mooring.
    And yet I yearn to see her under sail . . .
        gliding through the water as she was intended,
        strong and confident against the waves.

But before you up-anchor—tell me:
    For what port are you headed?
    Who is shipping off with you?

But most of all tell me:
    Why is your cargo so light?

When Love Shall Rise Up

When love shall rise up to pass the moon,
And catch the morning sun before its headbirth;
To set her light between two downstretched hands,
A path is forged down thruway, toll and bridge.
When love shall rise up its hands to the moon,
Move not, O sun, toward Gabaon,
Nor you, O moon, toward the valley of Ajalon—
Let time become blue lines on paper.
When love shall rise up to pass the moon,
And find there a hunter with rifle in hand;
Let her follow the sun into the night,
Leaving each hand to hold its head.
When bitches at last have slammed the bedroom door,
Then let jackasses serve up the rights of war.

Why the Motorcycle?

Why the motorcycle? she asked.
?Why normal be

It's the cooling rush of the breeze
against your body.
The clean smell of the air
when no one's in front of you.

You see what you've never seen before,
with no windshield, posts or
radio chatter in your way.

It's an effortless romp on a sunny day.

Or there's the excitement of taking the curves.
Lean back and down today
and take the 25 MPH curve at 40.
Tomorrow we'll try it at 45.

?Shouldn't I be working without a net

A Woman Who Can Whistle

A woman who can whistle
      Can have her way with me;
I'm a sucker for a woman
      Who can whistle in harmony.

She can wet my whistle
      If nothing else, this'll
melt me. But if doing a sloppy job
      Then she can go whistle.

A virtuoso performance
      And my foolish heart skips;
If performed both by puckered
      And pinky proffered lips.

I jerk to a whistlestop
      If I hear a shrill, clear note;
But only if that music
      Rises from a woman's throat.

Whistling to me she'll not be
      Whistling jigs to a milestone;
Nor will she be whistling in the dark
      For she will knock me prone.

So love, don't waste your time
      Whistling for your beer;
Make a sound clear as a whistle,
      And I will undoubtedly be there.

Wordly Separation

the words refuse to adhere to the page
like magnets with too much paper between
slipping down the front of a refrigerator

this inability, this depression . . .
is more a humming numbness than heart-pumping pain:
the feeling that overcomes you watching
the dust settle in a newly, permanently, emptied room
the confidence you feel staring down an empty subway platform
the silence that follows the killing of a cricket
the smile of a mind ripped loose from reality

i cannot write because, for me,
this world has been purged of its living
straight, painted walls,
level, swept floors . . .
it baffles me that when
we defecate we hide it beneath the streets
and sanitize and sanitize it
until its of no use to those living
and it piles up

a sanity built on such sanitization is
as clean as the shoulder high
inside of a subway door,
as dirty as an old lady's upper lip

Yet Again Today

I longed to talk to you
      Yet again today . . .   to hear your voice.
I wanted to tell you about
      loneliness and longing . . .   the familiar cadence.
How images of you
      gently form in my mind . . .   your honest laugh.

We never have enough time for the conversations
I have with you when I'm by myself,
walking the beach,
               tinkering at odd jobs
waiting for the subway.
Even so, you're my best companion
and a wonderful listener.

And then, when I see you,
      Like information overload, I cannot sort out
the rush and tumble of feelings;
      I am out of practice in love.

When did you become so important to me?
Why
     if my need to talk is so urgent
am I tongue-tied
     when I'm with you?
I'd rather soak you up than hear me.

All the hopes I ever had
      That never came true!
All the confusion about what
      to do now!
I can't lose you.

Young, Skinny Kid

Young,
        Skinny kid, with fascination
                in his eyes,
Sits in the basement
at a long-abused wooden office desk,
swayback from years of holding a typewriter up.

Beside the black barrel-bodied
                        oil storage tank,
the desk and the boy are arranged in still life: he
Staring, staring, staring,
at the dirty green cement wall before him.
His fingers
        lightly
                rest on the keys of an
                        upright
                        manual
                        Smith-
                        Corona.
His thoughts are filled by the hard-on that fills his pants.

The desk, too, if filled—
with many buildings
he has written
although few people live there.
Most have jagged, broken
                        windows.

The morning sun
                gives color to the sky.
Soon it will warm
the dampness of the basement
into stifling humidity
but the smell of oil will remain.

He writes:
     "The world is mine
     Only in the mornings,
     When those who would know me
     Are still close-eyed;

     When the beauty of darkness
     Surrounds and soothes me,
     Masking the loneliness
     Of my competition."

He rolls it out,
         reads it,
and files it in the desk with the other
half-completed buildings

                  and he moans.

Strangeness fills the room
as a thickness of air
         settles upon him
and the oppression is heavy-felt.

He rolls in another sheet
and rapidly yells
from within the typewriter:
     "To hell with love:
     I'd much rather feel love
     Taunt and tense and never consumed
     Then consumed without caring!"

But he doesn't believe,
although he reads it again

and gets up to go masturbate.

Your Eyes

Your eyes
(where I wander)
Hold out for my taking
a better life
than any of the nights of the road.

Reflected through your eyes
(where I sleep)
My lover's hand—tied
to yours
like the snow of a hillside.

Your love
is my dearest poem.

Your Long Lean Body

Your long, lean body, muscles rippling in your legs
        reflected in the mirror
Stops me as I hurry down the hall.

Fixing your hair,
you expose your hard, dark red nipples
pointed towards the image of you:
Double-beauty.

I slide in behind you and
        wrap my arms around your breasts,
Pulling you against me.
You wrap your hands over mine and close your eyes.

Reflected in the mirror
        I see the
Black-and-blue marks
        where you bit me this morning,
like a vampire sucking life.

I slide my hands down
        feeling smooth skin over curves.

And then it's time to catch the train.

You're Right

You're right,
of course:
A moon (such as I am)
could never comprehend
a shooting star
(such as you are).

Shining; shimmering;
Sparkles trailing in your wake!
Cascading higher
against the black, uncaring frigid sky—
A court of handmaids standing at attention
to accent you,
Mere diamond chips of light
to your bright
whiteness!

As your path dominates my sky
I can feel you siphon
power from me,
Employing the field of gravity of my emotions
as your slingshot.
You pass near enough to affect both of us
(me you tire,
to you I give impetus)
But not close enough for me to capture you,
And if I did:
What good a burnt-out meteorite?

As you searchingly pass beyond my pull
you try to maintain
Your momentum,
Building upon the emotions
You've harvested

from others,
And it hurts
When you're forced to burn
Your own emotional fiber
To maintain your height.

And if sometimes you travel too far,
Burning bright,
And become spent,
then you sink beyond the horizon,
Losing your whiteness
To the color of a single emotion,
And, Oh, it is a deep, dark void
into which the following
of one emotion
will lead you.

Then you must enter a new atmosphere,
Gaining in your beauty and power,
until all heads crane to gaze at you.
One exhaulting glimpse is all that is required
for men to love you.

All the while
I witness your beautiful display
My own emotions do not fuel me.
I am held in check
by the expectations of those who depend upon me
to be in their sky
to help light their way
when it is dark.
But, God, I'm a feeble light!
Better than nothing, naturally,
so even when I'm straining
at the far regions of my orbit
to break free,
The greater force that they are
tugs at my coattails.
They see me turn back and are reassured.

All I can offer you is a wide-open sky
for you to use
to siphon my emotions
whenever you need them,
And write across that sky
every now and then
The fire that is yours—
The shooting star that you are.